AF361555

SPIRITUAL CARE IN AFRICAN RELIGIOUS CULTURES

SPIRITUAL CARE IN AFRICAN RELIGIOUS CULTURES

SACRED WISDOM FOR THE CARE OF PERSONS IN AN INTERCULTURAL WORLD

EMMANUEL Y. LARTEY

Foreword by Kofi Asare Opoku

GEORGETOWN UNIVERSITY PRESS / WASHINGTON, DC

The publisher is not responsible for third-party websites or their content. URL links were active at time of publication.

Library of Congress Cataloging-in-Publication Data

Names: Lartey, Emmanuel, 1954– author.
Title: Spiritual care in African religious cultures : sacred wisdom for the care of persons in an intercultural world / Emmanuel Yartekwei Lartey.
Other titles: Race, religion, and politics series.
Description: Washington, DC : Georgetown University Press, [2026] | Series: Race, religion, and politics series | Includes bibliographical references and index.
Identifiers: LCCN 2025020043 (print) | LCCN 2025020044 (ebook) | ISBN 9781647126902 (hardcover) | ISBN 9781647126919 (paperback) | ISBN 9781647126926 (ebook)
Subjects: LCSH: Spirituality—Africa. | Pastoral care—Africa. | Healing—Africa—Religious aspects. | Africa—Religion. | Africa—Religious life and customs.
Classification: LCC BL2462.5 .L37 2026 (print) | LCC BL2462.5 (ebook) | DDC 204.096--dc23/eng/20250510
LC record available at https://lccn.loc.gov/2025020043
LC ebook record available at https://lccn.loc.gov/2025020044

♾ This paper meets the requirements of ANSI/NISO Z39.48-1992 (Permanence of Paper).

EU GPSR Authorized Representative
LOGOS EUROPE, 9 rue Nicolas Poussin,
17000, LA ROCHELLE, France
Email: Contact@logoseurope.eu

27 26   9 8 7 6 5 4 3 2   First printing

Printed in the United States of America

Cover design by Nathan Putens
Interior design by Westchester Publishing Services

Dedicated to and in memory of
Nunmo Tete Amugi
(my paternal grandfather)

Christian Agbenyega Doku
(1894–1934)
(my maternal grandfather)

Doris Christiana Lartey (née Doku)
(1917–2000)
(my mother)

TABLE OF CONTENTS

FOREWORD

A brilliant African proverb says, "The progeny of a chameleon will never lose the ridge down its back," and, indeed, the Right Reverend Professor Emmanuel Yartekwei Lartey, a Methodist pastor and the Charles Howard Candler Professor of Pastoral Theology and Spiritual Care at the Candler School of Theology at Emory University in Atlanta, Georgia, has clearly demonstrated that he has not lost the hillocky, chameleonic ridge of his ancestors. His paternal grandfather, Nunmo Amugi, was a traditional priest-healer in the religious and cultural traditions of the Gã people of Ghana; and his maternal grandfather, Christian A. Doku, was a lay pastor and church planter in the Methodist Church of the Gold Coast, now Ghana. Although Dr. Lartey's venerable grandparents operated in different cultural and religious landscapes, they nevertheless consciously committed themselves to the ministering care of souls, and their grandson has followed in their footsteps.

Dr. Lartey has written the priceless and informative *Spiritual Care in African Religious Cultures: Sacred Wisdom for the Care of Persons in an Intercultural World*, and readers of this absorbing book will appreciate the undeniable relevance of African spirituality to the practice of the care of souls. This volume is a fundamentally valuable and substantial addition to studies of classical African religion, as the author prefers to call it, and it eminently deserves to be regarded as a remarkable theological enterprise.

The care of souls that this book deals with has its well-laid foundation in a religious tradition whose primary concern is for the well-being of humans in this world and not a preparation for eternal life after death. As Archbishop Peter Sarpong, of the Roman Catholic Archdiocese of Kumasi, Ghana, plainly put it, "The African's religion concerns his whole person, not just his soul. It helps him to have children, to get rich, to avoid sickness, to get back his health, to grow old and to prosper."[1] And because of classical African religion's orientation to this world and not to eternal life in the next, protagonists of religions that claim to be otherworldly and possessors of the only truth or final truth have tended to consign classical African religion to near insignificance and have described it as a demonic, satanic, and monstrous religion without any abiding values. And yet these same adherents have proven to be more worldly minded and have rapaciously sought worldly goods; worldly power, political and economic; and have clearly demonstrated that for them this is the only world there is. One would have thought that those who believe and teach that there is a better world than this would leave the goods of the world to those who know no better than to believe only in this world. An African proverb says, "When deeds speak, words are silent," and the deeds of those who teach about a better world than this have spoken louder than their words, however inspiring they may be.

The unsparing disparagement of classical African religion by those who claim to have the only truth, and write trenchantly and authoritatively about classical African religion, display woeful ignorance of the African wisdom heritage that could have guided them in their writing. Out of this heritage comes the adage, "Truth is like a baobab tree; one person's arms cannot embrace it," which means there is no religion that has arms long enough to embrace the baobab tree of truth, no single religion has a monopoly on all truth, and wisdom subtly recommends that to credibly succeed in surrounding the baobab tree of truth, religions should hold hands. Another epigram from the bubbling well of African wisdom says, "The wise person does not say that he/she has the final word, but the fool insists," which tacitly acknowledges human limitation and prudently cautions against the monopolistic tendency to lay extravagant claim to absolute or final truth. This is the wisdom heritage that made it possible for classical African religion to play host to the guest religions that came to Africa; and the fact remains that an objective appraisal of classical African religion can intelligently profit from African wisdom.

In the eight chapters of this illuminating book, the author discusses beliefs and practices of classical African religion from the perspective of practitioners who find meaning and significance in their lives in the spiritual traditions of their ancestors. This wholesome approach gives classical African religion a transparent integrity of its own and rescues it from the throttling grip of relentless misrepresentation.

In chapter 1, the author explores the nature of classical African religion and examines the worldview, which he prefers to call the world-sense, of African people. Chapter 2 takes the reader through the ritual activities that enable individuals to successfully navigate life's transitional points, while chapter 3 presents the reader with a discussion and reconceptualization of the phenomenon of "spirit possession," and draws on the views and experiences of practitioners themselves. In chapter 4, the author discusses beliefs and practices that address and respond to the palpable challenges to life and well-being of persons and communities—illness, misfortune, natural and human-caused disasters—that Africans face. And since the need for guidance through the vicissitudes of life's journey is recognized as basic to human life and development, chapter 5 describes forms of guidance through divination in classical African religion. In chapter six, the author explores the role and function of classical African religion in restoring the vitality of life and life force to persons and communities that have lost it. A discussion of funerary practices in Ancient Egypt as well as contemporary beliefs and practices of funerary rituals and customs follows in chapter 7; and the concluding chapter is a summary and articulation of the overall essence of spiritual care that emanates from the African worldview that is explored throughout the book.

Beliefs and practices of classical African religion are not uniform throughout the continent; there are differences in beliefs and practices, but they all arise out of the African experience and can therefore be rightly described as African. Divinity is essentially a spirit, without any visual representation, which points to its limitlessness. A person is not a representation of divinity; rather, the *Ɔkra* of the Akan of Ghana, which is the essence of a person, is part of the substance of *Ɔdomankoma*, the Creator; and that is why an Adinkra symbol of the Akan says, "I will die only if God dies." Since God does not die, the *Ɔkra*, which is part of the substance of God, does not die. A person, therefore, is essentially a spirit, Ɔkra in a human body, *nipadua,*—hence the Akan name for a person, *Ɔkra teasefo*, a spirit that is living or a spirit that is encased in a body, nipadua. It is the body that dies, but a person is not their body; death, therefore, does not end life. Life is indestructible and has no opposite; it is constant. Birth, therefore, is the entry gate and, death, the exit gate, through which life passes to renew itself. It is birth and death that are opposite, not life and death.

Nature or the world around humans is not at the "feet" of humans (as the Psalmist says in Psalm 8:6, "Thou hast put all things under his feet."'); rather, it is a society of living beings, or an extended family of which humans are a part. And classical African religion led to the development of an environmental ethic that laid marked emphasis on harmony and respect for nature. This attitude reflects a deep understanding of nature that expressed itself in a feeling of reverence for the multitudinous forms and forces of the natural environment.

Professor Lartey eminently deserves commendation for writing a book about the spiritual care of persons in continental African and African diasporan communities in line with classical African religious traditions, and for opening readers' eyes to the wealth of knowledge embedded in these traditions, which are part of humanity's quest for meaning in life. Dr. Lartey has eloquently given clarity of meaning to the African proverb, "Hunt in every forest, for there is wisdom and good hunting in all of them."

Professor Kofi Asare Opoku,
Easton, Pennsylvania,
June 2025

Professor Opoku is the former director of the Institute of African Studies at the University of Ghana and of the Kwabena Nketia Centre for Africana Studies at the African University of Communications and Business.

Notes

1. Peter Sarpong, "Ghanaians and their culture: Rites de Passage," *Catholic Voice* 46, no. 2 (1971): 23.

ACKNOWLEDGMENTS

This book began as a series of lectures I gave as a part of a course titled African Religious Traditions and Healing, which I had the pleasure of co-teaching with my Emory colleague Professor Dianne M. Stewart, beginning in 2006. I later reconfigured and expanded the course and taught it with the designation that forms the title of the book—Spiritual Care in African Religious Cultures. My thanks go to Emory and Candler graduate students who have taken these courses down through the years. Thanks are due to Iyalosa Omolewa, Reverend Dr. Salim Faraji, Iya Dr Fulanyo Wood, Dr. Rachel Harding, Reverend Dr. Melanie Harris, and Reverend Dr. Lahronda Little, each of whom has contributed to the teaching of the course, and through several productive conversations to the crafting of the book. In this regard, mention should also be made of Akua Baakan and Wanjiku Gachugi for your stimulating input stemming from your practices of African religion.

My professor, mentor, and teacher, Professor Kofi Asare Opoku, deserves special mention, as does African mystic Bro Ishmael Tetteh. Both of you have specially inspired and sustained me along the arduous journey of writing, providing me with stellar examples of pure African religious practice.

This book is dedicated to the memory of three of my illustrious ancestors. Nunmo Tete Amugi, my paternal grandfather, was a priest/healer and a practitioner of classic Gã religion. My maternal grandfather, Christian Agbenyega Doku, was a Methodist lay pastor and church planter. My mother, Doris Christiana "Korko" Lartey, introduced me to an openness to and recognition of the rich variety and nuances of religious traditions and practices that may enhance any individual's well-being. Though long departed, they all deserve loud praise for the contents of this text.

This is my first book to be published by Georgetown University Press (GUP). I am exceedingly grateful to Terrence L. Johnson of Harvard Divinity School for recognizing the value of the book proposal and first introducing me and this project to GUP. Great thanks are due Alfred "Al" Bertrand, director of GUP until his untimely death in April 2025, who shepherded the project, received the manuscript in August 2024, and began the process of production. Elizabeth Sheridan-Drake continued overseeing the production of the book and deserves much thanks for seeing it through to publication. I would also like to acknowledge and thank Hope LeGro, Kacie Greenfield, Jasmine Zhang, Francys Reed, and all of GUP for your part in bringing this book into print.

Unfailing thanks to my life partner Griselda and family members, Theo and Ellen, Emilia, Liam; Henry and Boo; Jai and Renee, Isaiah, Aniyah; Wesley, and Sara, without whom I would have been unable to complete the work of writing the book.

Introduction

M Y PATERNAL GRANDFATHER, NUŊMO AMUGI, was a traditional healer, spiritual consultant, town maker, and community leader. He founded a sacred village, established a shrine (healing center) there, and operated in the court of the local chief as a guide, priest, and adviser. Stories of his effective employment of herbal remedies as well as his efficacious spiritual consultations have been shared with me by many relatives and community members. He was a highly regarded "priest-healer" within the religious and cultural traditions of the Gã peoples who live within the environs of Accra, now the capital city of Ghana. My maternal grandfather, Christian A. Doku, was a catechist (lay pastor and church planter) in the Methodist Church (in the then Gold Coast). He is recorded as having planted many of the Methodist churches in the coastal towns west of Accra. My mother accompanied him on many of his evangelical journeys, carrying his bible on her head and performing as lead singer during worship and outreach services. He died when my mother was only nineteen years old and a student in a teacher training college. I am exceedingly blessed to have been given many firsthand accounts of his life and ministry by my mother as well as through scouring the official records of the Methodist Church in Accra.[1] As I write about the care of persons in African life and thought, I am conscious of being the inheritor of the heritage and vocations of these two illustrious ancestors, both of whom, out of their different religious and cultural traditions, left substantial legacies of practices of care for persons. I have profound respect for and draw consciously as well as unconsciously on all my classical African religious heritage, practiced by Nuŋmo Amugi, as well as the vibrant African Christian life and practice of Christian A. Doku, the church planter. In a manner of speaking, these two traditions course through my physical and spiritual veins and are in evidence in practically all my previous publications and works in the field of spiritual care, albeit unacknowledged explicitly.

In most religious traditions, there is typically encouragement for practitioners to be attentive to the needs, suffering, and concerns of people. The love of and care for others seem to be basic and essential tenets of humanity's highest endeavors. Spirituality, in its many varied forms, reaches its most valuable expression when it uplifts the practitioner and those around, deepening their sense of selfhood and developing their ability to be helpful to all of humanity.

A hallmark of the oft-denigrated classic continental African religious and spiritual traditions is a primary concern for the well-being and promotion of life of persons and communities. The most highly spiritually developed person, adept and steeped in the highest of sacred practices, is in African cultures understood to be the one who is able through their spiritual arts to bring about material and physical blessing and benefit to the human community. In traditional Africa, spirituality is linked inextricably to the well-being and flourishing of the human community. African moral philosopher and theologian Laurenti Magesa followed his fellow Tanzanian Roman Catholic theologian Charles Nyamiti in arguing that "African religious behavior is centered mainly on man's (sic) life in this world, with the consequence that religion is chiefly functional, or a means to serve people to acquire earthly goods (life, health, fecundity, wealth, power and the like) and to maintain social cohesion and order."[2] The ultimate test and criterion of authenticity of a priest or healer in African religion is not doctrinal but rather practical. Authenticity boils down to the question of the efficacy of their spiritual practice: Can this person reverse negative circumstances and transform them into beneficial ones? Can they heal the sick? Can they secure bountiful harvests? Do they know of or possess the ability to orchestrate fecundity for the barren? Do they have the power to procure profitability for the entrepreneur? Do their spiritual practices ultimately bring benefit to the human community?

The sharp dichotomy within westernized thought between the sacred and the secular, the material and the spiritual, the physical and the ethereal, is largely absent from traditional Africa. Rather, in African life and thought, all of life is sacred. The different aspects of life cohere, interpenetrate, are interrelated, and influence each other. There is no part of human life that is not animated by the life forces of creation. The sacred is not divorced from the secular. The spiritual person is of great benefit to the total well-being of the human community. The life lived on this very material earth is not compartmentalized. Every aspect of human living pulsates with the rhythms of the unseen realm.

In this book I examine how spiritual care is conceptualized and practiced in continental African and African diasporan communities in line with classic African religious traditions. I seek to explore, from the perspectives of practitioners of these traditions themselves, those beliefs and practices that originate and are operative on the African continent as well as in other parts of the world, which orient African and African-descended persons toward wholeness and well-being. The main objective of this text is to make clear the thinking that underlies the practices of spiritual care that arise from and within African religious life and thought. In Western scholarship African religions have most often been studied under the nomenclature of "African traditional religions." In this book I will be speaking of them as classic African religions (CARs). These religious and spiritual beliefs and practices are "classic" in at least two senses: first, because of their antiquity—they have been in existence and practice for millennia; second, they reflect an original essence; in other words they represent the core understandings and seminal practices from which many derivations and tributaries have developed.

Spiritual Care from the Perspective of Classic African Religion

By "spiritual care" I mean the utilization of means and methods that are related to the spirituality of persons in the pursuit of the total well-being of people and communities. Spiritual care refers to how people draw on their own spiritual traditions and those of the people they serve to help them live satisfying and productive lives. Spiritual care practitioners employ practices such as prayer, meditation, counseling, divination, mediation, rites of passage, worship, teaching, ritual, and preaching, among others, to assist persons in their quest for wholeness and wellness in their lives. This book seeks to draw out principles of spiritual care that are based on the beliefs and practices of practitioners of classic African "traditional" religion. It is therefore not a book about Christian pastoral or spiritual care. Instead of deriving principles of care from Western Christian teachings or doctrines, I have delved into the traditional religions of Africa to draw out what spiritual care might look like if it was premised on those beliefs and practices. In keeping with African understandings of the holistic nature of human life, African practitioners of spiritual care pay attention not only to a narrowly defined "spiritual" or "religious" aspect that to them is in any case not divorced from the "secular" aspects of their lives, but rather to *all dimensions* of people's lives including the social, interpersonal, emotional, physical, economic, cultural, cognitive, political, as well as religious. African spiritual care providers are deeply respectful of people's spiritual and religious sentiments, beliefs, and practices, and while attentive to potentially harmful aspects of these, do not assume that all such beliefs and practices are necessarily evasive, toxic, or pathogenic. Rather, African spiritual care practitioners pay close attention to how these activities may be harnessed for the well-being and welfare of all people.

Worldwide studies of pastoral and spiritual care have repeatedly indicated that such care is engaged typically to achieve goals such as *healing, sustaining, guiding, reconciling, nurturing, liberating, and empowering*[3] for individual persons as well as for communities. Through a careful examination of practices that seek to achieve these outcomes within African communities, I will be exploring spiritual care insights that arise from African religious life and thought, thus illustrating African religion's nature and value. Moreover, I shall also be exploring African practices and beliefs that are geared toward the total well-being of all persons and communities. *Spiritual Care in African Religious Cultur*es as such gives valuable information about African spirituality, African religious and cultural beliefs and practices, and the purposes they serve. Such knowledge can be crucial in the provision of human care services in multicultural communities across the world.

It is a well-known fact that both popular Christianity and Islam, the two religious traditions demographically most practiced on the African continent, show evidence of the incorporation of African culture, beliefs, and practices within them. Over the years as a pastor, teacher, and care provider, I have practiced forms of pastoral and spiritual care among persons of African descent living in Europe, North America, and the Caribbean, within so called "immigrant" congregations as well as in educational and social institutions. Out of that experience I can state categorically that *lived religion* among African peoples worldwide is very often an amalgam of different traditions, beliefs, and practices.[4] Consequently, in this text I do not ignore popular Christianity and Islam among African peoples but rather refer to, expose, and explore the dynamic integrations and interactions of the diverse religious and cultural traditions they represent. Throughout the book you will find that I have paid close attention to African and African-diasporan lived religion in its many-sided pluriformity and variety.

The Study of African Religion

As previously stated, this book is not primarily about Christian pastoral care, but rather about spiritual care derived from the beliefs and practices of classic African religion. The study and articulation of African religion by Christian missionaries and leaders has very correctly been severely criticized.[5] Christian and Islamic functionaries have often done a great disservice to African religion, culture, and traditions, belittling, demonizing, ridiculing, and distorting them historically under the guise of "civilizing" the African, or most often to serve their interests of "conversion."[6] Within what can only be described as a white supremacist framework, all things African or non-European have been deemed uncivilized, inferior, demonic, or simply evil. I agree very much with the critique of Otok P'Bitek and recognize the denigration of African culture, life, and thought that Christians and Muslims have perpetrated. Consequently, counter to and in critique of that Christian history, I have made every attempt as a practicing Christian myself to pursue my engagement with African religion with the utmost regard for and recognition of the distinct differences that exist between African religion, Christianity, and Islam. A guiding principle in my work is articulated well by Thomas when he writes, "Any methodology used to analyze, observe, or pass judgment upon ATR (i.e., African Traditional Religion) must use tools and assessment measures that are developed from within the tradition."[7]

Through exposure to the practices of classic African religion on a day-to-day basis as well as through research and study, very much like Agbonkhianmeghe Orobator, "I have experienced it up close and personal and have learned to understand, respect, critique and appreciate its values and practices."[8]

Consequently, my approach to African religion has been to privilege the voice and views of practitioners above every other theory or perspective. I have sought to let continental as well as diasporic African practitioners of these religious traditions explain the inner logic and their emic understandings of the practices they engage in for the care of the people they serve. I have attempted at all points neither to impose Christian insights on African realities nor to compare them with each other. I have sought to privilege and prioritize African concepts and practices as expressed by practitioners of African religions.

Large numbers of Africans and African-descended peoples live in virtually every region of the world. I spent fifteen years living, studying, and teaching in the United Kingdom and Europe. I have also spent the last twenty-four years living and working in the United States. Based on reflection on my experiences, in this book I seek to give vital information on practices of care that find synergy among African peoples wherever they may be currently located. Multicultural communities across the world will find here information on African ways of being in the world as well as African understandings and practices of spiritual care. Such information can prove useful in enhancing public health and relational well-being in all communities across the world.

My primary aim in writing the book coincides with one of the stated objectives of my fellow African Christian, Agbonkhianmeghe Orobator, in writing his book *Religion and Faith in Africa: Confessions of an Animist*. A Jesuit priest and practitioner of African religion, Orobator seeks "to retrieve African Religion as a repository of wisdom and practical insight for the spiritual renewal of all people through its endless quest for meaning, purpose, and wholeness."[9]

Though this book is not primarily intended to articulate Christian pastoral care, it can be of value to practitioners of Christian pastoral care in at least two significant ways. First, it dispenses with the pervasive sense among African Christians, especially of an evangelical persuasion, that African religion and culture is in essence evil, demonic, or else harmful and destined only to ultimately destroy its practitioners. This view is not only patently false but is also harmful to the God-given sense of identity and dignity that Africans, *qua* Africans, have. African religion has been the host culture—and a very hospitable one at that—for Christianity and Islam on the continent. It has been the seedbed of and continues to provide the conceptual and communal framework within which these two faiths have been able to grow and thrive into the dynamic and dominant global forces they are now. Classic African religion has much to offer believers of any faith tradition. It is high time African Muslims and Christians gave African religion its due in terms of respect and recognition.

Second, it highlights the differences that exist between Western Christianity and African "traditional" religion, thereby resisting the attempts by some Christian scholars to obscure these differences ostensibly to Christianize and hence "dignify" African customs and beliefs. Though there are areas of similarity, African religion has its own theological, cosmological, eschatological, and ethical understandings that are distinct and different from Western Christianity. African religion does not need to be contorted into Christian form for it to be acceptable. Christians and Muslims need to recognize and respect the distinct values, precepts, and practices of African religion as having its own authentic and distinct place within and among the varieties of global religions. Christians can usefully and fruitfully engage in respectful dialogue with African religionists on the basis of a recognition of difference rather than an assumption of similarity or a presumption of superiority.

Chapter Outline

Chapter 1 explores the nature of African religion.[10] This entails a discussion of the world-sense,[11] beliefs, and practices of practitioners of African religion.

Sacred ritual holds a central place in African religious consciousness. Ritual, far from being seen as routine activity repeated to serve mundane everyday purposes, is engaged as crucial for interaction between the seen physical world and an unseen spiritual reality. Recent popular usage of the term in West African contexts would suggest that "ritualists" are people who employ human sacrifice (dubbed "ritual") in their quest for material, especially financial gain. Chapter 2 centers on ritual in its more ancient classic African sense and explores how ritual is understood and engaged in African religious communities for the benefit of individuals and communities. Illustrative *rites de passage* surrounding birth and death are explained with a focus on how these rituals operate as a means of conveying persons from one stage of life to the next. Here we gain a deeper understanding of the interconnectedness of spiritual activities and human flourishing, especially how spiritual activities can enable successful navigation of life's transitional points.

One of the most visible and expressive aspects of African spiritual experience has been termed "spirit possession" by anthropologists and by Western and westernized observers and commentators on African religion. This description, like many others of African religious experience, hardly coincides with the views of practitioners of these religious traditions and those who have experienced the phenomenon. Chapter 3 discusses and reconceptualizes the phenomenon, drawing especially on the views and expressions of practitioners themselves who have such experiences.

Illness, misfortune, natural and human-caused disasters, and other personal, social, and communal ills present human beings with real challenges as they pose obstacles to human life and flourishing. In chapter 4 there is a discussion of beliefs and practices that address and respond to the palpable challenges to life and well-being of persons and communities that Africans face. I attempt to explore the role of human, ancestral, and spiritual agency in the causation as well as relief of these challenges, obstacles, and obstructions to the free flowing of life and health.

The need for guidance through the vicissitudes of life's journey is recognized as basic to human life and development. Chapter 5 discusses forms of guidance through divination in African religion and how these serve the functions of spiritual direction and divine guidance for persons and communities facing the bewildering varieties of choices and decisions humans must make in the world. It is also an expectation that religious leaders and people who claim divine inspiration will have knowledge or means to such knowledge that can serve others in helping them avoid mistakes, dangers, and misdirection in life. Religious practitioners, especially spiritual leaders and adepts, are typically sought out regarding this function of guidance.

Chapter 6 explores the role and function of African religion in restoring the vitality of life and life force to persons and communities in whom this has been lost or has waned. This entails an exploration of African healing systems, including concepts of disease, health, and healing; beliefs about various illnesses; and various healing practices of African traditional healers. Given the emphasis on social and relational dynamics in African life and thought, the social implications of these beliefs and practices of healing and health care are given prominence.

Chapter 7 takes us into one of the most visible features and expressions of African social life and thought, namely death and funerary practices. Social and historical research has unearthed lines of connection and similar thought partners across the continent of Africa when it comes to death, ancestral traditions, and funerary practices. Drawing on Ancient Egyptian funerary beliefs, practices, and writings, as well as contemporary rituals and customs surrounding death, this chapter reflects on beliefs, rites, and practices associated with transitions to the ancestral realm. A discussion of the nature and function of ancestors is also engaged in this chapter.

Chapter 8 is an articulation of the particularities of spiritual care that emanates from the African world-sense explored throughout the book. It expresses in summary what spiritual care emanating from African consciousness and spirituality looks like, how it functions, and what it accomplishes.

Each chapter is characterized by an emphasis on the beliefs and practices that practitioners of African religious traditions engage in with the express purpose of providing spiritual care for persons and communities. In considering each aspect and focus identified in each chapter, attention is paid to how it contributes to the well-being of practitioners and the entire human community. The main purpose of the conclusion is to outline major lessons learned and implications for the spiritual care of persons influenced by African spiritual and religious beliefs and practices throughout the entire world.

Notes

1. See Rt. Rev. Dr. Seth A. Aryee, *History of the Establishment and Expansion of the Methodist Church, Ghana: Greater Accra, Eastern, Volta Regions. 1838–1978.* (Unpublished).
2. Laurenti Magesa, *African Religion* (Orbis, 1997), 51.
3. For explanations of these functions, see Emmanuel Y. Lartey, *In Living Color* (Jessica Kingsley, 2003), 60–68.
4. For many examples and case studies that have arisen out of that experience, see Emmanuel Lartey, *Pastoral Theology in an Intercultural World* (Wipf and Stock, 2013).
5. Perhaps the most trenchant has been by Okot P'Bitek. See Okot P'Bitek, *Decolonizing African Religions* (Diasporic Africa Press, 2011).
6. For a fulsome critique of Western, Christian, and Islamic attitudes toward African Religion, see Douglas Thomas, *African Traditional Religion in the Modern World* (McFarland, 2015), 44–98.
7. Thomas, *African Traditional Religion*, endnote 1, 263.
8. Agbonhianmeghe E. Orabator, *Religion and Faith in Africa: Confessions of an Animist* (Orbis, 2018), 22.
9. Orobator, *Religion and Faith in Africa*, xvi.
10. Despite many obvious differences and particularities that are evident in African communities about religious beliefs and practices, many dispassionate observers and practitioners make mention of the broad themes and similarities that are observable by those who take more than a cursory look at the fascinating complexities. As such I prefer to speak about African "religion" in the singular, whose main tenets can be compared with Islam, Christianity, Buddhism, and other "world religions."
11. Oyeronke Oyewumi defines "world-sense" as an inclusive way of describing the conception of the world by different cultural groups. She uses the term in describing the Yoruba and other cultures that privilege senses "other than the visual or even a combination of senses." *The Invention of Women: Making an African Sense of Western Gender Discourses* (University of Minneapolis Press, 1997), 3.

1

Nature of African Religion

"African traditional religion is a way of being in the world.[1]"

AFRICAN RELIGION HAS BEEN VARIOUSLY understood, categorized, and theorized about by different scholars and thinkers. These lines of thought have run the gamut from there being no such thing as African religion ("Africans have no soul," no ability to conceptualize such a complex reality as divinity), through plurality (African religions—each tribe has a distinct and entirely Indigenous set of practices that are unintelligible to others), and on to there being nothing in the African's consciousness but religion (seen as "superstition"). African peoples have thus been characterized widely as, on the one hand, "having no religion," to, on the other, being "incurably religious."[2] Such extremes and polarities point to a basic misunderstanding of the nature and function of African religion within African communities on the part of some Africans and those non-Africans who have sought to study or write about it.

Practitioners of classic African religion speak of their practice as being a way of life, imperceptibly interwoven with the normal day-to-day activities by which we all live. Religion, as Magesa presents it, is not like the clothes we put on and take off but rather like the skin in which we live. For the African person there is no ontological atheism. The very fact of life and humans being in existence bespeaks the reality of Being—the God who is Being itself—and the ground of all being. The life force of the Creator pulsates through the veins of every living being, including the animals and all of nature—trees, rivers, rocks, mountains, the ocean, and the skies. Africans balk at the concept of religion as a set of doctrines formulated for purposes of assent and intellectual belief. African religion could be and often has been reduced, very often by Christian scholars, to a set of beliefs. But African religion is far more than this. Moreover, it cannot simply be reduced to patterns of belief. Classic African religion is understood by its reflective practitioners as a spirituality for living, providing the fuel for fruitful and successful navigation of a complex and difficult world fraught with dangers and challenges. Tanzanian Roman Catholic scholar Laurenti Magesa captures it well when he declares, "It is a 'way of life' or life itself, where a distinction or separation is not made between religion and other areas of human existence."[3]

To deepen our understanding of the practices of spiritual care that are engaged in by practitioners of African and African-diasporic religious traditions, let us now consider ten overarching themes that run through and emerge out of African religious living amidst its varieties of expression.

All of Life Is Sacred

Rosemary Clark, who has engaged extensively with the traditions of Ancient Egypt, writes,

> The ancient Egyptians did not see a rift between the workings of the divine and mundane spheres. The sacred encompassed the secular in their world view; the physical world—including natural phenomena and the plant and animal kingdoms—was seen as a reflection of the divine world, and everything in it possessed a divine nature. The gods manifested through the visible—human beings, trees, stars, wind, and storm, even though these living things possessed an identity of their own as well.[4]

In classic African religious belief, the divine is immanent in nature. God's presence is discernible in all the earth. An ancient

African sacred text from the time of Rameses II describes this thus:

> The soul of Shu is the air, the soul of Neheh is the rain,
> The soul of Ra is the primeval ocean.
> The soul of Asar is the ram of Mendes,
> The soul of Sobekh is the crocodile.
> The soul of every god resides in serpents,
> The soul of Ra is found throughout the land.
> —The Book of the Celestial Cow, Dynasty 19.[5]

Divine energy flows through all of nature. The material earth is infused with the presence of the divine. Nothing in life is free from the imprint of the Creator. All of life pulsates with the rhythms of the unseen world. In West Africa, the Akan peoples of Ghana and La Côte D'Ivoire have a saying, "Nsem nyinaa ne Nyame," which may be translated as "all matters are connected to or originate with God." Laurenti Magesa further states the pervasive sacrality of the African world this way; "At all times in a person's life, a religious consciousness is always explicitly or implicitly present."[6] In writing about African spirituality, Magesa appropriately gives his book the question *What is not sacred?*[7] for its title. He writes, "In Africa, there is an essentially 'transcendental' perception of all life, because all reality is situated in the sacred realm, which is the spiritual sphere. A people's life is their religion, so that 'religion' or 'spirituality' is not a separate institution but rather an intrinsic and inseparable part of a whole life."[8] In reality, for "Africans religion is quite literally life and life is religion."[9]

Magesa articulates three essential characteristics that make up this view of life: "first, all existence consists of energy or power."[10] Various terms have been applied to this energy such as life force, vital force, divine life. Magesa explains, "it consists of active, existential forces that continually and consistently interact with and influence one another (for good or evil). Through these relationships, all existence (and specifically human life) becomes possible."[11] Second, Magesa continues, "all creatures participate in the comprehensive power of life, each to a different degree, at their own level within the whole."[12] In this way he underscores the belief in the shared nature of life between the different forms of life characteristic of African thought. Third, in an expressly anthropocentric turn, he writes that "all vital energies existing in the universe, that is, the spirit of existence, coalesce to serve human life."[13] To speak of African "religion," then, is to speak of the permeating energy or force that makes all of life possible and real.

African Religion Is "This-Worldly"

Africana religious scholar Elana Jefferson-Tatum argues that classifying religion, especially Africana religion, as the "metaphysical," "spiritual," "otherworldly," or "unseen" aspect of life is patently wrongheaded. She argues, "Africana orientational worlds exemplify a non-transcendental metaphysics wherein nature, 'spirits,' matter, and 'humanity' fundamentally coexist and commune, and wherein *matter* is the essential 'stuff' of religion."[14] Jefferson-Tatum continues, "within Africana-sacred landscapes the metaphysical is made *real, material,* and even *active* through the natural."[15] She argues that "in many Africana religious cultures, divine forces and energies are understood as operative and active within *this* world. There is often, no otherworldly domain—no realm set apart from the realities of this world. Rather, the divine realm is a parallel and overlapping cosmos that is constantly concerned with and engaged in this-worldly concerns, problems, and experiences."[16] With reference to the work of her mentor, Bernard Adjibodou, spiritual chief of the town of Adjarra in Porto-Novo, Benin, Jefferson-Tatum takes pains to point out that "*vodun, orisa, lwa,* and other similar, effectual, ontological entities cannot be separated from the matters and materialities of nature and the natural world. Rather, these powerful entities are made concrete, perceptible, and perceivable through their materialization into empowered shrines, statues, devotees, and other organic and even seemingly inorganic bodies—whether a wooden *vodun*, an activated *nkondi*, a *nganga* pot, a consecrated *ori*, or even *otanes*."[17]

Time and Space Are Sacred

Within classic African religion all time and space are sacred. Time is sacred because it is linked with life. Past, present, and future are linked imperceptibly together. Child-naming ceremonies celebrate this connectedness through the fact that newborn children are typically given the names of their ancestors in the strong belief that children are reincarnated souls of their ancestors. As will be more fully explored in chapter 2, this linkage with the past is then underscored in these ceremonies, which are conducted at the first light of dawn to coincide with the rising of the sun and thus to symbolize that the newness is linked with the sun and stars whose age-old existence is recognized every day at their rising. Linked to this is also the future enshrined in the prayers and ideals held before the child, who is instructed to grow up living a life that embodies these ideals.

Of space, Magesa declares, "All space is sacred because its physical, material appearance contains the invisible powers that make life possible: the world of spirits is integrated into that of space."[18]

A fundamental tenet, then, of classic African religion is a highly developed sense of the sacrality of life and of everything that is in existence. Africans inhabit and operate within a sacred universe. Nothing is merely *secular* without any ultimate significance. All things reflect and bear the energetic stamp of their existence.

The World as We Know It Is Constituted of Two Powerful Interpenetrating and Complex Realms

In an African world-sense, there is a visible or "seen" realm that comprises the physical world experienced by humans through sensory means. There is also a parallel world, an invisible or "unseen" realm, that is the divine, ancestral, unconscious, or "spiritual" world. These two realms constitute reality as the African perceives it. They interact with and interpenetrate each other. As such, it is important to understand that in classical African awareness these realms, though distinguishable, are not separable. They are distinct only for the purposes of conceptualization, discussion, and recognition.

Sacred rituals and ceremonies, as we shall discuss more fully in chapter 2, are frequently the means by which the interaction of the realms is enacted and engaged. Inhabitants and participants in the unseen realm retain the potential of being in interaction with people and things in the seen realm. Spiritual practices are often employed to facilitate entry by people in the seen realms into the unseen realms and to experience the unseen while retaining firm grounding within the seen one. Spiritual practices, such as prayer, and ritual activities, are typically the ways to engage the two realms and have them work together for the benefit of people and the human community. The training and work of priests, spiritual leaders, healers, and other religious functionaries takes place largely within the liminal space between the two realms. Adepts of classic African religion are those who have learned the art and science of fostering the interpenetration of the two realms in ways that benefit the community of people, especially those who inhabit the "seen" realm. Nevertheless, it is important to note that some ritual activity is also directed at benefiting those who inhabit the unseen world.

Plurality and Complexity Exist in Both Visible and Invisible Realms

Just as there are many different forms of life on the natural, physical (seen) plane, so also are there different forms of existence in the invisible (unseen) realm. Variety, plurality, and complexity exist fully in each realm. Nature comprising humans, animals, plants, rivers, mountains, and other material or physical phenomena are present on the physical plane. Ancestors, deities, divine beings, spirits, and other entities populate and operate from the unseen realm. As previously argued, these two realms interpenetrate and are in interaction at all points in time. In classic African religion animals, plants, rivers, and mountains are all also "inspirited," having spiritual essences that animate their physical existence. Jefferson-Tatum makes this very important observation that underscores the inappropriateness of the widely used descriptions of a "natural" and "supernatural" world, with spirits or deities occupying the "supernatural" one. She writes: "While scholars often label African 'gods' and 'spirits' as 'supernatural,' these entities and forces are neither otherworldly nor transcend nature. Instead, nature is their abode; it is the landscape and medium of their familiar bond with the visible world."[19] In classic African religion the distinction between a "natural" and a "supernatural" realm is meaningless. All of the natural world is infused with supernatural energy, and all of the "supernatural" world operates within the natural realm. The only distinction that makes any sense is that between what is visible in a material sense and what is invisible in that sense.

"Gods," "Deities," and "Spiritual Entities"
Are Divine Principles

An important often overlooked understanding of the entities referred to as deities, divinities, gods, or goddesses is that in African consciousness, these terms are also ways of speaking about principles or natural laws.

The Ancient Egyptian *neteru* are cosmic principles, laws, and forces of nature.[20] They are the personifications of the energies that pervade the whole universe. Similarly, the *orishas* of Yoruba religion are personifications of natural forces and cosmic principles. Classic African religion accounts for principles of life and natural forces through the postulation of spiritual entities inhabiting the parallel universe of the unseen world. For example,

Ma'at is an ancient Egyptian goddess who personified the concepts of truth, justice, balance, order, and harmony. She was also associated with law and morality. Oshun is the Yoruba goddess (orisha) of love, beauty, and fertility.

Rituals and religious practices are geared toward facilitating interaction between the realms, and the enactment of the ideals and principles of the life personified by the deities within the seen world.

Spirituality Is at the Center of Our Human Existence

From an African perspective, at the core of African anthropologies lies a central organizing aspect of the human personality variously designated -*okra*- Akan; *kla*- Gã; *ka*- Ancient Egypt; *ori*-Yoruba, which refers to a God-given essence that is received or uniquely chosen in the divine realm prior to a human being's entry on earth. This spiritual inner reality serves as the core of or key driving force of a human being's life purpose, character, or personality. This component of a human being links one with the divine essence while also being the core of one's personality. Humans, to employ an expression attributed to French Jesuit, scientist, paleontologist, theologian, philosopher, and teacher Pierre Teilhard de Chardin, are in essence spiritual beings having an earthly or physical experience. Any approach to the care of persons within an African environment that does not address this central feature, or that has nothing to offer that dimension of a person's experience, is fundamentally flawed and doomed to failure. Spirituality, rather than psychology, is the central dimension to human existence that needs to be attended to in the care of people.

For Magesa, "Spirituality can be described as the process of interaction between thought and behavior and the visible and invisible existences surrounding humanity."[21] There is a vital connection between spirituality and life itself. Magesa continues, "spirituality in Africa is not extraneous to the totality of the life of the individual or the community and the universe. It cannot be conceived of as having an existence detached from total involvement in the created order. Rather, spirituality in Africa is seen as human participation in the total universal existence, the whole of human existential experience in the world. It is embedded in the entire being of people and things."[22] As such, Magesa is rightly insistent that "Humanity must constantly interact intelligently and compassionately with all spiritual powers for its own good and that of the entire universe."[23] This is the art and science of classic African religion. Adepts facilitate this intelligent and compassionate interaction with "spiritual powers" of various sorts. Spirituality, in classic African terms, far from being something arcane or esoteric, is "perhaps the one thing that is *really* real, not merely a conceptual idea. On the contrary, it is the most experiential reality in the totality of being."[24]

Personhood Is Defined Relationally

African concepts of personhood are deeply relational. The Zulu characterization of persons with the phrase *Umuntu ngumuntu ngabantu,* which literally means that a person is a person through other people, exemplifies relationality as foundational to personhood. "Ubuntu" means "I am, because you are."

Akan anthropology describes humans as comprising the following components:

- *Okra* (which may be translated as "spirit") that is received from God prior to birth.
- *Mogya* (literally meaning "blood" in Akan language), received from mother, and mother's lineage.
- *Sunsum* (which could be translated "soul"), is received from father and represents an educable and flexible aspect of humanity which can be made stronger or weaker by experience, training, or challenges of life.

- The physical body is known as *Nipadua* (literally "person-tree") and is the earthy, natural edifice that each person possesses and inhabits for the duration of their sojourn on the earth plane. Each anthropological term in Akan is therefore relational.

One's *okra* relates one with the Creator. One's *mogya* is the maternal relational dimension. *Sunsum* relates one with one's father, and *nipadua* speaks of one's relationship with the earth.

The African approach to existence is as such thoroughly personalist. Magesa argues that "for African personalist spirituality, the energy of life . . . though invisible, is always embodied, personalized, or personified in some form or manner. Spiritual agency is always integrated in and with elements of the universe, and human existence and agency are interconnected with transcendent and immanent reality."[25]

The late Ghanaian theologian and Anglican clergyman Professor John Pobee characterizes the essence of African being, in contrast to Descartes' *cogito ergo sum* ("I think therefore I am"), in terms of the Latin expression *cognatus ergo sum*, which means "I am related by blood, therefore, I exist."[26] By this means Pobee highlights the fact that in classic African thinking the core idea of being is relational. In other words, we are relational beings through and through. A person is a locus of relationships and is to be understood as such.

To construe African community as "collectivist" with no place for the individual is to miss the point of the relational nature of African anthropology. The Akan concept of *okra* as well as the Yoruba notion of *ori* (spiritual inner head) point to a deep consciousness of the uniqueness of each person. These concepts show that a person's singular individuality is highly valued. In fact, this feature of humanity is the divine Creator's gift to each person, known and owned solely by the specific individual to whom it is given, or better still, negotiated between the person and the Creator. It is a mark, perhaps the highest mark, of "individuality."

African persons, then, in Akan and Yoruba culture and mythology, individually work out and create a unique "inner head" or "personal spirit" with which they enter the seen realm. Each person's life on earth is then a discovering and living out of the individual trajectory (in Akan, *nkrabea*) that they personally worked out with the Creator prior to their birth. This life plan, purpose, or destiny is known only to the individual head or spirit.

Human Life Is a Composite, Synthetic Whole

Every human is a multidimensional being made up of parts that are held together in a gestalt whole that is much more than the sum of its parts. This classically African view of personhood can be characterized as *relational holism*.[27] Each aspect of human essence, as we have seen, is relational. Additionally, each is related to other inhabitants of the realms of existence in a cosmos that is relationally defined and constituted. Each facet of human being, as identified by the Akan peoples of Ghana and La Côte D'Ivoire, is held in relationship to the other by divine energy in a bond that makes for unity. The binding force of community is precisely this divine energy called life. The whole cosmos is thus a network of relationships that need to be in harmony and balance for health and well-being to exist.

Religion scholar Douglas Thomas makes this fundamental truth abundantly clear: "There is nothing within the [African] traditional purview which exists in isolation, including humans, animals, plants, or stones. Isolation equals death. All things are intricately connected to an overarching worldview."[28] To be isolated or cut off from this network is to essentially be rendered nonexistent.

Harmony Throughout the Cosmos Is Crucial for Human and Communal Well-Being

Priests, healers, traditionalists, and practitioners of African religion unite around the idea that harmony is a crucial characteristic of well-being. Thomas recognizes this significant central piece of classic African religion when he makes the following statement: "The maintenance of communal and cosmic harmony is the hallmark of African traditional religion."[29] Connoisseurs and practitioners of this religious orientation to life make this the rhyme and reason of their entire practice.

Magesa makes it clear that, "although the spiritual power of the universe is always greater than any of its constituent parts, and although each part only makes complete sense in the context of the greater universal whole, the principle that makes life, indeed, all creation possible, is 'interdependence,' 'mutuality,' and complementarity. Nothing can live or even exist on its own. The universe exists on account of its component parts and vice versa, and each creature needs the rest in the delicate balance of existence."[30] Priests and practitioners cherish and work for this "delicate balance of existence."

Harmonious existence is earnestly sought within classic African cultures and communities. Here, health and well-being are fundamentally understood as harmony and balance. Magesa presents it this way: "In the worldview of practically all African cultures the exchange of energies as a necessary condition for the possibility of all existence involves, most importantly, the well-being of the human vital energy and is necessary for the well-being of the rest of the created order. In a sense, the welfare of the universe depends on the health of human beings."[31] In recognition of humanity as the apogee of creation and most consciously expressive of the divine life on the visible plane, Magesa goes on to assert, "human beings bear ultimate responsibility for universal harmony because they represent creation as conscious of itself, its most manifest spirit. By disturbing the equilibrium of the universe, humanity eventually destroys itself, meaning that the fate of humanity and the rest of the universe are inseparable."[32]

"The task of the village diviner," Magesa continues, "and all other community leaders . . . is to make sure that the requirement of proper existential exchange of vital forces in the universe is maintained. The balance of energies between humans, the spirits, and other creatures must not be upset."[33]

The fullest expression of African religious life and thought, then, is that which promotes living in harmony with all things in existence. The *orisha, lwa,* and *neteru* are primarily forces of nature that assist persons to live at peace with all things. All practitioners of African religion in its classic form would agree with Thomas that "maintaining cosmic harmony with all things in existence is the *modus operandi* of African traditional religion. Harmony among human beings, animals, nature, and the divinities is vital for maintaining peace in life. Imbalance is a disorder or 'sin' that must immediately be dealt with. If not, chaos will pursue those who are out of alignment with the forces of life."[34] In sum, then, "African religion is a spiritual system that aims at restoring cosmic balance between human and nonhuman entities."[35]

Ritual Connects the Realms of Existence

Rituals in the form of prayers, pouring of libation, sacrifices, offerings, drumming, rhythmic bodily movements, dance, herbal baths, and ingesting food or drink, among others, are liturgical means through which the human, the natural, and the divine realms are brought significantly into interaction. Rituals are life-giving and are participated in with total body-mind-soul consciousness and attention. Rituals creatively symbolize and celebrate our participation in what we long for and mystically connect us with the divine. In classic African ritual, "the rhythmic language of the drum and the bodily movement of the dance are the media through which mystic connectivity is enacted."[36]

In Ancient Egypt sacred ritual was performed to maintain the relationship between humanity and divinity. As Rosemary Clark observes, "rituals were recreations of the acts of divine beings when life arose in the beginning of time. And the performance of rites was regarded not only as a high calling, but a spiritual exchange that offered countless benefits to the participant."

An early inscription on a statute found at a temple dedicated to the deity Amun declares:

> To the prophets, divine fathers, priests, and lectors
> And all who enter Amun's temple of Ipet Sout:
> By performing the rites and making the offerings,
> By doing the service of the month priest,
> The great god will give you life.
> You will be flawless in his presence,
> You will be fortified with his blessings.
> —Inscription on the statue of Harwa, Dynasty 25[37]

Sacrifices and Offerings

By far the most evident ritual in shrines as well as everyday rites of practitioners of classic African religion are animal sacrifices. John Mbiti maintains that sacrifices "are acts restoring the ontological balance between God and man, the spirits and man, and the departed and the living."[38]

Sacrifices are the primary means by which classical Africans maintain and restore relations with the divine, ancestors, and the community, and as such aim at restoring communal balance throughout the entire cosmos.

Understood theologically, sacrifices are a medium used to restore and maintain communal relations. Sacrifice, in that understanding, is a form of petition to higher forces. Much the same as prayer in other traditions, Thomas states that, "sacrifices are a mode of communication between the visible and invisible worlds."[39]

Adeyemo studied notions of salvation in classic African religious communities. Writing about sacrifices and offerings, he declares, "traditionally, sacrifices and offerings are believed to be a means of contact between man (sic) and the deity. They are said to be man's (sic) best way of maintaining an established relationship between himself and his object of worship."[40]

Thomas distinguishes among at least four major types of sacrifices and offerings in traditional African communities as follows:

- Meal and drink offerings, performed daily at shrines and on festive or sacred days.
- Thank offerings, daily rituals that express one's appreciation to a deity for bringing success to one's family.
- Propitiatory offerings and sacrifices, aimed at averting communal catastrophe or crisis.
- Vicarious sacrificial offerings, conducted to undo offenses committed against a divinity.

Thomas rightly concludes that sacrifices and rituals in general in traditional African cultures "speak to the people's desire to maintain communal and cosmic relations with all of creation."[41]

A Sense of Belonging Is Crucial for Personal and Communal Well-Being

Participation in communal life can be understood as the essence of African traditional being. To be is to belong to an identifiable network of relationships held together by a strong sense of belonging. This sense of being a part of a whole can be fostered through ritual participation and the promotion of interpersonal relationships. A classic example of this can be found in the naming ceremonies that are traditionally held for newborn children.[42]

Such powerful ritualizing of belonging has a lasting impact on individuals as well as the entire community. Moreover, the fact of giving the newborn a name in accordance with the naming system of the family serves to imprint on the child an identity that is carried for the rest of their lives.

Names typically are given from the ancestral heritage of each family. The repertoire of names associated with specific families means that children can be identified as belonging to specific families and ethnic groups simply by the mention of their names. In this way names become not only marks of identity but also signs of belonging in families. To have a name is to belong to a family and thus to have an identifiable place within an ethnic group. Naming thus gives identity, place, and belonging to each individual person.

My own name is an example of a misnomer in the African sense. My father was an only child of his mother. He was sent off to school—a Methodist mission elementary school in Accra, Ghana—to acquire an education and means of social uplift- ment. At registration each pupil's name is recorded in a class register. On his first day at school and without the presence of mother or father, my father mentioned the name he had re- ceived by virtue of his family of origin—YARTEY. The English missionary teacher retorted, "I don't know and have never heard that kind of name before." He wrote down LARTEY—a name he had heard before and that seemed to him more like what it should be. From that point on, therefore, my father was called LARTEY, and this is the name that was handed down to all his children as ours. What had just happened was highly significant. The missionary had by the stroke of his pen dis- lodged a whole family of people for generations from their place of belonging within their extended family and forcibly associated them with a different family to which they did not belong. Anyone who knows the naming system will immedi- ately recognize the anomaly. A Yartekwei (my middle name) cannot be a "Lartey"! *Yartekwei* can only be a son (third-born son, to be specific) of a "Yartey." Larteys are an entirely differ- ent family group.

African Religion Is Pragmatic and Life-Affirming

The overriding goal of classic African religion is the well-being of the human community. African spirituality's primary aim is the promotion of communal well-being. The most spiritual, religiously able, or highly "developed" person is the one who is able to interact with the unseen world in ways that are beneficial to the visible living community. Indeed, the mark or test of one's spirituality lies in the ability to help, heal, bless, feed, or clothe and shelter the needy within the human community, through one's interactions with the unseen world. Such leaders are traditionally "elders" in their communities.

Each spiritually adept person can by vocation and training become a minister of or specialist of a certain deity. Typically, they are also healers who possess deep knowledge of herbal pharmacology. Ministers of classic African religion, then, are dispensers of sacred knowledge and have access to secrets to healing of various sicknesses and diseases. As Thomas puts it, such people "are the recognized masters of a sacred grove or of a place of worship."[43]

Classic African religion aims to promote life and to enhance the flourishing of all humans. It is a practice far more than a set of ideas. It is action-oriented and evaluated by the people in terms of its efficacy. Spiritual care is its essential character, nature, and purpose. Its practices, wherever in the world they are found, aim to provide well-being and health for all practitioners and participants.

Notes

1 Douglas Thomas, *African Traditional Religion in the Modern World* (McFarland, 2015), 154.
2. Philosopher Willy Abraham and African Christian scholar of religion John Mbiti have both presented this view.
3. Laurenti Magesa, *African Religion* (Orbis, 1997), 25.
4. Rosemary Clark, *The Sacred Magic of Ancient Egypt* (Llewellyn, 2003), 2.
5. Clark, *The Sacred Magic of Ancient Egypt*, 3.
6. Magesa, *African Religion*, 58.
7. Laurenti Magesa, *What Is Not Sacred? African Spirituality* (Orbis, 2013).

8. Magesa, *What Is Not Sacred?*, 24.

9. Magesa, *African Religion*, 26.

10. Magesa, *What Is Not Sacred?*, 33.

11. Magesa, *What Is Not Sacred?*, 33.

12. Magesa, *What Is Not Sacred?*, 33.

13. Magesa, *What Is Not Sacred?*, 33.

14. Elana Jefferson-Tatum, "Africana Sacred Matters: Religious Materialities in Africa, the Caribbean, and the Americas," in *Earthly Things: Immanence, New Materialisms, and Planetary Thinking*, ed. Karen Bray, Heather Eaton, and Whitney Bauman (Fordham University Press, 2023), 61.

15. Jefferson-Tatum, *Earthly Things*, 65.

16. Jefferson-Tatum, *Earthly Things*, 67.

17. Jefferson-Tatum, *Earthly Things*, 69.

18. Magesa, *What Is Not Sacred?*, 58.

19. Jefferson-Tatum, *Earthly Things*, 66.

20. The singular term is *neter* and the plural *neteru*.

21. Magesa, *What Is Not Sacred?*, 28.

22. Magesa, *What Is Not Sacred?*, 40.

23. Magesa, *What Is Not Sacred?*, 40

24. Magesa, *What Is Not Sacred?*, 41.

25. Magesa, *What Is Not Sacred?*, 40.

26. John S. Pobee, *Toward an African Theology* (Abingdon, 1979), 49.

27. For further elaboration of this classically African view of personhood, see Emmanuel E. Lartey and Hellena Moon, eds., *Postcolonial Images of Spiritual Care: Challenges of Care in a Neoliberal Age* (Wipf and Stock, 2020), 21.

28. Thomas, *African Traditional Religion in the Modern World*, 95.

29. Thomas, *African Traditional Religion in the Modern World*, 186.

30. Magesa, *What Is Not Sacred?*, 33–34.

31. Magesa, *What Is Not Sacred?*, 29.

32. Magesa, *What Is Not Sacred?*, 29

33. Magesa, *What Is Not Sacred?*, 29

34. Thomas, *African Traditional Religion in the Modern World*, 181.

35. Thomas, *African Traditional Religion in the Modern World*, 201.

36. Emmanuel Lartey, *Postcolonializing God: An African Practical Theology* (SCM, 2013), 28.

37. Clark, *The Sacred Magic of Ancient Egypt*, 4.

38. John Mbiti, *Concepts of God in Africa* (SPCK, 1970), 179.

39. Thomas, *African Traditional Religion in the Modern World*, 20.

40. Tokunboh Adeyemo, *Salvation in African Tradition* (Evangel, 1997), 33.

41. Thomas, *African Traditional Religion in the Modern World*, 20–21.
42. See chapter 2 for an example of prayers and rites that are typically performed at these ceremonies.
43. Thomas, *African Traditional Religion in the Modern World*, 97.

2

Ritual

Sacred Technology of African
Religious Cultures

"**R**ITUAL IS CENTRAL TO VILLAGE life, for it provides the focus and energy that holds the community together, and it provides the kind of healing that the community most needs to survive."[1]

As a young minister in Ghana in the early 1980s I came across several customs and practices associated with life transitions that were deeply entrenched within the culture of our folk. Especially striking were funerary rites that were practiced without exception as mandatory. When I asked about the origin and reason why these practices were necessary, I was consistently told that is the way we have always done these things. "We inherited them from our ancestors." Much later I began to study Ancient Egyptian customs only to find these customs recorded, engraved, and inscribed on temple, tomb, and pyramid walls.

Ancient Egyptians had developed what has been termed "Sacred Science" believed to have influenced many ancient cultures including the Persian, Greek, and Roman. Egyptian creation legends communicate that the spiritual objective of this ancient science was "realizing and maintaining the harmony among gods, nature, and human beings."[2] Clark explains that "the means to accomplishing this interaction between the life streams was a time-honored, spiritual technology that was believed to have been given to the human race by divine beings."

The rites, rituals, and ceremonies of Ancient Egypt are known now to be among the most ancient and "probably the most effective in achieving its spiritual goal—maintaining the bonds between the human, divine, and natural worlds."[3]

Clark argues, "one of the implications of this spiritual technology—Sacred Science—was the transformation of the human form into a vehicle for higher functions. In the words of the Egyptians, it was a process of 'making gods.' This profound goal is reflected in the knowledge that was employed to further its process."[4] Three distinct but interconnected ways of creating gods have been identified. These are described as "esoteric architecture, cosmic resonance, and theurgy."[5]

Esoteric Architecture

Ancient Egyptians, astute observers and recorders of nature and natural occurrences as they were, employed numerology, geometry, measures found in natural forms, and mathematical models based on their observations of the movement of the sun, moon, and stars. These ancient African peoples have left a legacy of an intricate approach to constructing temples, tombs, and pyramids that also included the use of symbolic art and unique building materials. Sacred principles drawn from nature are encrypted in the monuments and buildings they crafted. The layout of every shrine was an emulation of the natural landscape of creation. The "house of a god," whether shrine or temple, was designed and crafted as a mirror image of the god (most often depicted as the personification of a natural energy source like sun, moon or plant) in its domain in celestial regions, and the chambers, halls, and passages represented functions of the deity at rest, active manifestation, and pro-creation. The crafting of shrines, temples, and coffins to carry the mortal remains of men and women are today constructed to reflect this belief. If in life a person was, say, a craftsperson, a sailor, a pilot, a carpenter, or an engineer, then in death their coffin is crafted to depict their status, profession, or what they loved to do.

Cosmic Resonance

In the Ancient Egyptian worldview, far from being random or obtuse, nature is organized and intelligent. These ancient Africans practiced a sacred astronomy—that is, they observed celestial events in context with their connection to and influence on terrestrial life. This stemmed from their belief that divine forces reside in all natural phenomena—the sun, moon, planets, stars—and that their rhythmic appearances mark significant events for other living beings. They carefully studied the relationship between cosmic events and earthly occurrences with a clear belief that what happened in the heavens had a palpable effect on what happened on the earth. As above, so below. Ancient Egyptians developed the practice of invoking and communicating with divine forces at specific times indicated by their observations of the movements and positioning of the stars and planets.

Theurgy

Ancient Egyptian priests and royals developed and sought to perfect the practice of the performance of Divine work. The Ancient Egyptian word Heka, meaning a powerful spoken word that materializes what is named, was understood also as the name of a deity. The divine command "let there be light" (in Genesis 1:3) is a prime example of the creative impulse enshrined in sound, word, and naming. This notion of powerful word is both a sensory function and a divinely regulated action that forms the underpinnings of African spiritual practice. We know that in ancient African culture, spiritual practice was sensate and expressed through sacramental forms of ritual. All the conscious faculties were employed toward this end, including sight, sound, scent, taste, and feeling. In addition, special knowledge was transmitted through the physical vehicles of the religion—the art and architecture of the temples—and through symbols, color, spatial harmonics, and carefully selected materials for dress and ceremony. In turn, all these elements were designed for use in episodes dictated by cosmic timing—in cycles determined by the day, month, and year.

Clark captures the essence of ancient African ritual performance by pinpointing its aim in this way: "The purpose of this elaborate system was aimed to synchronize the senses of mortals with the phenomena of the natural landscape, both visible and invisible. It was believed that in this manner, the unity between the three lifestreams could be experienced and, most importantly, maintained."[6]

This exemplifies the understanding that African ritual at core exists for connectivity's sake. The many and varied rituals that are celebrated and engaged in in African life are all about establishing and maintaining connection throughout the world and between the realms of existence.

Ritual: Being in Connection

Africans historically affirm that in order to live well it is necessary for us as humans to maintain the connection between the living, the dead, and the unborn. To flourish we must connect the seen with the unseen, the physical with the spiritual, the human with the divine.

Typically, every ritual entails relating and connecting the *three* dimensions of our existence:

NATURE (earth, air, fire, water, mineral)
THE HUMAN (human beings, society, community)
THE UNSEEN (divine, spiritual beings, ancestors)

African medicine man, philosopher, and diviner Malidoma Somé sums this up very well: "The purpose of ritual is to create harmony between the human world and the world of the gods, ancestors, and nature."[7]

Ritual harnesses the energies of the natural and human world in communicating with the unseen, divine world. In ritual these three realms of existence are brought into vital relationship with each other. Great energy is released whenever the realms are connected and communicate with each other.

Ritual: Language of the Divine Realm

Ritual is the language of the gods, the language of the unseen realm articulated through the material and symbols of the seen realm. Each deity, spiritual entity, each ancestor or spirit, has its own ritual that essentially is a form of language they understand and communicate in. To communicate with any spiritual entity, one must "speak their language," so to speak. This is why one needs to learn to practice different rituals and thus speak to different entities. Moreover, different rituals exist to address different circumstances of life. There are rituals of invocation, healing, reconciliation, peacemaking, warring, fertility, divining, seeking guidance, strengthening, and protection, to name only a few. Each of these purposes are related to and governed by specific deities. As such, just as one learns specific languages to communicate with people of different countries or ethnicities, so one has to discover or be led to the right forms of ritual pertaining to the circumstance and deity related to the circumstance, which communicates with the deity and unlocks the required energies to address the circumstance.

Ritual Transforms

One of the most important differences between African notions and practices of ritual and that of the Westerner is that for the African, "ritual is a spiritually powerful means of effecting change in both the seen and the unseen world."[8]

African ritual is not simply routine customary practice that has little or no significance beyond lubrication of personal and social life. For the African, ritual changes things in very significant ways. Malidoma Somé makes this abundantly clear:

> If something in the physical world is experiencing instability, it is because its energetic correspondent [in the unseen realm] has been experiencing instability. People go to that unseen energetic place to try to repair whatever damage or disturbances are being done there, knowing that if things are healed there, things will be healed here. Ritual is the principal tool used to approach that unseen world in a way that will rearrange the structure of the physical world and bring about material transformation.[9]

As we shall be discussing more fully in chapter 6, in African life and thought, illness is a condition that must be addressed through ritual.

As already mentioned, there are different types of rituals practiced for different purposes and at different times. Offerings and sacrifices serve as the principal means of communication with, gifts to, and prayers to the unseen divine realm. They are often engaged in times of crisis or performed daily to ensure harmony and peace within families and communities. Sacrifices and offerings are also employed to make amends and requests, or to show gratitude for all our blessings.

Senegalese and African American authors Adama and Naomi Doumbia explain the essence and spirit of sacrifices and offerings in classic African life:

> When we make an offering or sacrifice, we give up something that has significance for us in our daily lives. These honorable acts teach us the value of what we have and what we are able to share. We learn from our offerings and sacrifice the true

meaning of our blessings. This cultivates our humility and gratitude, which invites more blessings our way. Sometimes we give our offerings to the spirits directly, sometimes we give them to people in honor of the spirits. We give that which will bring joy to others. We give to others, and they pray on our behalf.[10]

Ritual as Propitiation

Adama and Naomi Doumbia address a crucial function that ritual performs in human communities: "We often make an offering or sacrifice to amend our disruptive ways. If we harm those in our communities, creatures in our environment, or elements of nature, we make an offering to appease the *nyama* (i.e., life force) of the transgression. When one harms any member of the community or any living being, including plants and animals, one must make the appropriate offering to atone for the violation."[11]

Community, reciprocity, and spirituality are the undergirding values of ritual engagement and practice in classic African life. They are the raison d'être and the rhythm of ritual practice and are criteria by which rituals in contemporary society can be evaluated and utilized.

Let us now consider an African rite of passage ritual that embodies and portrays essential characteristics of ritual in African religious cultures.

A Birth Ritual: Welcoming, Incorporating, and Inspiring New Members of African Community

As we hinted at in the last chapter, an example of the child-naming rites widely practiced among West Africans highlights the essential elements and ingredients of ritual performance in classic African culture and religion.

Gã "Outdooring" and Naming Ritual

The Gã people[12] of Southeast Ghana have traditionally performed a carefully crafted ritual of naming for newborn infants in their communities. Termed "outdooring" ceremonies among the Gã people of Ghana, every child born is *outdoored* and *named* traditionally at dawn on the eighth day after they are born—to coincide with the day of the week on which they were born. Officiants at these ceremonies are representatives of the families of paternal and maternal grandparents. Each represents a part of the heritage and physical bloodline of the child. Outdooring ceremonies include prayers in the form of libation, and statements that are spoken out in the presence of the child and the assembled community aimed at encouraging the child to know that they belong to an extended community. These statements are declarations of the values and ideals of the community that are to be imbibed and practiced by the newborn members. Through these ceremonies families embrace their newborns, and newborns are engrafted into them.

The ceremony is dubbed an outdooring for the infant because historically it represented the first time the child was taken outdoors.

Men and women representing the four branches of the child's kindred assemble in the open courtyard of the (father's) family house before daybreak. The infant is brought from its mother's house by a matri-kinswoman.

The ceremony begins with the presentation of a bottle of liquor by the infant's paternal relatives, and a pot of ŋmaadaa (corn drink) by the maternal relatives. A coin is symbolically placed underneath the pot or calabash of drink signifying the preparedness of the relatives to "carry" (in other words, nurse and train) the child for life.

Invocation of Ancestors

The senior patri-kinsman pours a libation invoking the presence of the ancestors at each door of the house, moving from right to left (and counterclockwise). The final act of this invocation of ancestors is libation (prayer) at the main entrance to the house.

A woman from the paternal house uses a fresh broom to sweep a spot of the floor of the courtyard where the infant will be laid. In the natural (this-worldly) sense the significance of this act is that it cleanses and cleans the area. Its spiritual significance is that it sweeps away forces of evil, misfortune, and death.

The baby, wrapped in a blanket, is brought out of the room and handed to the principal officiant (PO). The PO is normally the same gender as the child and is selected for their virtuous character. The belief in this is that the officiant's touch influences the child's character.

Presentation to the Heavens and Impartation

The PO stands facing eastward. At the first light of dawn the PO lifts the child up toward the morning star, symbol of the Supreme Being; places the child on the prepared ground (three times); and prays as follows:

> *Agooo! awomei ke ataamei* (3X) Gathering response:
>> *(Amee)*
>
> Hail! mothers and fathers [Yes, we hear you]
> What is Today? Today is. . . . . . (the day of birth, e.g.,
>> Saturday)
>
> Grandfather's Saturday and Grandmother's Saturday
> Lo, the stranger who has come,
> We are showing her/him to the morning star.
> Wind blows before a Gã person speaks,
> He sees, he has not seen.

> He hears, he has not heard.
> No lying, no stealing, no false witnessing.
> Father is father and mother is mother.
> Today we are presenting you to the morning star.
> Come and work that you may eat.

The third time the PO lays the infant on the ground and sprinkles water (symbolizing rain, blessing, well-being) on them. The PO then takes the child in their arms and puts three drops of corn drink on the baby's tongue, admonishing them to remember the obligation to maintain the cardinal virtues of Gã culture. The PO then gently kicks the child with their left foot saying, "I am striking you with my foot" (meaning, "I am impressing my character on you"); and then kicking the child with the right foot saying, "Take hold of my foot" (meaning "become like me").

Outdooring Prayer

The outdooring prayer, the central act of the entire ceremony, is then recited by the PO, with all gathered responding at the end of each injunction with "Hiao" (= "Yes, indeed!" or "Let it be so"). The prayer in translation:

> Hail, Hail, Hail!! Let *Omanye* (well-being and gladness) come.
> Are our voices one? (3X)
> Hail, let well-being come.
> The stranger who has come, his/her back is towards the darkness
> Their face is toward the Light.
> May they work for their father
> May they work for their mother
> May they not steal,
> May they not be wicked,

The children of this family forgive everything that can be
    forgiven.
May they eat by the work of their five fingers
May they come to respect the world
Upon their mother's head, Life!
Upon their father's head, Life!
If we should join up to make a circle,
May our chain be complete
May our brooms be thick
If we dig a well, may we come upon water.
If we draw water to bathe our joints, may they be
    refreshed.
If we see white clay, may it be white clay.
They came with black (hair)
May they return with white (hair)
Hail! Hail! Hail! Let *omanye* clothe us.
Are our voices one?
Hail! Let *omanye* come upon us.

The Naming Rite

The "naming drink" (liquor) is then presented by the patrikin.
The PO announces the child's name. The drink is poured into a
glass and passed around the circle. Everyone mentions the child's
name before taking a sip of the drink. By drinking the naming
drink and repeating the baby's name, each participant acknowledges that they have witnessed the naming of the child and
thereby assumed responsibility for assisting in the child's up-
bringing. The "stranger" has thus become a full member of the
family with their own name. No longer is the newborn a stranger;
they are now an integral part of a visible human family with an
individual name that signifies and portrays their belonging and
place within the family.

Concluding Prayers and Celebration

Gifts are presented and words of counsel given. Any member of the community is free to share words of advice to the parents and family members on community living and child raising.

The ritual ends with concluding prayers (libation) and a hand-rubbing rite. The celebrants rub their palms together three times, placing them on their right shoulders; they rub their palms three times again and place them on their left shoulders; finally, they rub the palms together three times and place them on their breasts.

The ceremony is then crowned with feasting and merrymaking involving all the gathered community of relatives and well-wishers.

Community, Reciprocity, and Spirituality

Outdooring and naming rites strengthen community relations by gathering people together to welcome newly arrived members, and by holding communal values before the eyes of the infant as well as the entire gathered community. The roles assigned to maternal and paternal relatives in the provision of required drinks, preparation of grounds, and invocation of ancestors, as well as the gender alignment of the principal officiant with the infant, all bespeak the reciprocity Gã people cherish. The prayers and symbolic impartation of character portray the importance the people give to good character and moral living, which are seen as pathways to ancestorhood. The naming itself invokes and reminds the community of the continued presence of the ancestors. The entire ritual portrays and celebrates the closeness, communion, and connection between the earthly human family and the unseen heavenly one. This, then, is a significant example of the function and purpose of African ritual in strengthening the life of the human community.

Notes

1. Malidoma Patrice Somé, *Healing Wisdom of Africa: Finding Life Purpose Through Nature, Ritual, and Community* (TarcherPerigree, 1999), 24.
2. Rosemary Clark, *The Sacred Magic of Ancient Egypt: The Spiritual Practice Restored* (Llewellyn Publications, 2003), 20.
3. Clark, *Sacred Magic*, 21.
4. Clark, *Sacred Magic*, 22.
5. Clark, *Sacred Magic*, 22.
6. Clark, *Sacred Magic*, 22–23.
7. Malidoma Patrice Somé, *Of Water and the Spirit* (Penguin, 1994), 32.
8. Emmanuel Lartey, *Postcolonializing God: An African Practical Theology* (SCM Press, 2013), 43.
9. Somé, *Healing Wisdom of Africa*, 23.
10. Adama Doumbia and Naomi Doumbia, eds., *The Way of the Elders: West African Spirituality & Tradition* (Llewellyn, 2004), 19–20.
11. Doumbia and Doumbia, *The Way of the Elders*, 20.
12. My father is Gã by ethnicity and heritage. My mother is of Dangbe ethnicity. Linguistically, the Gã-Dangbe speak the Kwa languages Gã and Dangbe and are a patrilineal people. Dangme is exclusively closer to the original Gã–Dangme languages than the Ga language.

3

Manifestation of Spirit

Elevated State of Consciousness

IN A SEMINAL STUDY PUBLISHED in the early 1970s, cultural anthropologist and documentary filmmaker and professor Sheila Walker set out the most significant parameters for understanding the phenomenon of spirit possession, which, she correctly states, "has existed in most areas of the world down through history."[1] Walker argues that for "possession" to be properly understood it has to be studied from various disciplinary perspectives since no simple singular explanation appears adequate to explain its complexity. In her monograph *Ceremonial Spirit Possession in Africa and Afro-America*, she considers the phenomenon from neurophysiological, hypnotic, psychological, sociological, and cultural deterministic viewpoints, noting that it is necessary "to consider the various factors involved, both singly and in conjunction with each other." She continues, "these factors need not all function together in all instances, but the particular factors involved determine the character of the manifestation."[2]

Walker's study focuses on "traditional societies in which there is communal ceremonial possession of individuals by specific deities or spirits who impart their particular personalities and behavior to the individuals possessed."[3] This approach prioritizes the perspectives and explanations of the "traditional communities" themselves as having the greatest import. My approach in this book places the same value on the emic perspective, and privileges the experiences and explanations of people who have themselves experienced the phenomenon and who can therefore speak from within the experience.

In this respect Walker makes a relevant distinction between the terms "possession" and "trance." "Trance," she argues, "is the scientific description of a psychological and physiological state in Western terminology, whereas possession is the folk explanation, in more philosophical terms, for the same type of state." With affirmative reference to an earlier study by Anthony Wallace, Walker defines possession as "any native theory which explains any event of human behavior as being the result of the physical presence in a human body of an alien spirit which takes control of the host's executive functions, most frequently speech and control of the skeletal musculature."[4] The emphasis on the presence of an alien spirit or deity is also evident in John Beattie's work referred to by Walker. "Beattie stresses the individual's state of dissociation or auto-hypnosis, or claim to illness, and the society's explanation of what it recognizes as unusual behavior as due to the control of an outside agent who either inspires the individual to act in a particular manner or displaces the individual's personality and acts in its stead."[5]

Manifestation Rather than Possession

All participants in religious activities in which spirit possession is evident, in my experience, do indeed attribute the observable behaviors of the possessed to the presence of an alien deity or spirit. It is the manifestation of the deity or spirit that results in the behavior in question. However, by far the language of description preferred by these participants and those who have experienced the phenomenon is not "possession" but rather *manifestation*. The physical state in question is the direct result of the manifestation of a spiritual entity within the human body of the recipient. The possessed demonstrably *manifest* and express through their body the nature, presence, and activities of the spirit in question.

The accounts of Haitian musician and researcher Mimerose Beaubrun come closest to what I have heard from participants in the complex and fascinating experience of possession.[6] For her and for the many from whom I have heard, what they experience is a *materialization of lwa,* or a *dream-state while awake.* In explaining possession this view is that among a variety of states of consciousness that we as human beings can experience, this is one of them, and it results from and is induced by the manifestation of a deity or spirit.

In terms of Haitian social existence, Beaubrun focuses her study and interest in the *lakou,* which she explains is "a kind of vital space, a place of multidimensional life where several families, or rather, an extended family, shares all aspects of life (spiritual, economic, cultural)."[7]

Aunt Tansia, the adept and mentor who initiated both Mimerose and her husband Lolo into vodun, is the one being referred to in this explanation:

> "The structure of the lakou," she told me, "is designed in accord with the <u>state of consciousness</u> of the founder; that is, it is based on a direct rapport with the unknown world, which can only be reached through trance. There are different degrees of trance. There are trances so deep that the *chwal* (individual possessed by a lwa) can spend a month or more outside himself. There is the inspirational trance that writers, musicians, poets and artists in general are familiar with. There is the trance in which one sees and hears the spirits, the one that dreamers know. The trance of ecstasy in which one travels through distant regions in full consciousness. The ecstatic trance that the *dòktè fèy* (leaf doctor, or healer) knows, in which the initiate acts lucidly while his spirit communicates at the same time with other spirits."[8]

For those who have experienced the phenomenon, then, there are different levels, durations, and purposes for the manifestation of spirit referred to as possession or trance. What it calls for, therefore, from a spiritual care perspective is attention to the degree of intensity, the length of time, as well as the goals to which any such experience is directed. Spiritual care purveyors themselves frequently experience these states and practice their care directly under the inspiration of the manifesting spirits or else are given direction or instruction during these states concerning how to offer help to those needing it.

Elevation of Consciousness

Altered States of Consciousness: Encounter of Worlds

Mimerose Beaubrun gives us a most personal, vivid, and illustrative account of the experience under study:

> I didn't move, but, in an instant, I lost all sense of continuity. I was both conscious and unconscious at the same time. I moved between two states, completely whole at one and the same time in these two parallel worlds. I saw myself standing up in the place where I was before, and at the same time I saw myself perched on the *poto mitan* [i.e., the middle pillar, principal axis in the center of the Vodou peristyle, symbolizing the encounter of two worlds: the spiritual world and the material, physical one (sky and earth)]. I don't know how long it lasted. . . . I was filled with new energy. I had no doubt about the animating force behind it. But I had no desire to talk about it. I had understood something for which I had no explanation that could be put into words.[9]

Beaubrun's descriptions give some access to the depths of the experience of spirit manifestation. Beyond the ordinary physical and material life we all experience as human beings, Beaubrun explains that Haitian vodou recognizes at least three other forms of consciousness. The first is described as *je klè* and explained as "open-eyed, or possessing consciousness.

A concept that defines the first level of attention; the faculty of seeing and distinguishing material, physical and visible things."[10] A second is known as *nan dòmi,* "a concept that defines the second level of attention. One enters into a state that permits one to see abstract things unknown until then. A lucid dream state."[11] Then, thirdly, there is *pinga-pye* (literally, "watch out for your feet"), "a concept that defines the state which is above the first and the second level of attention. It is the state of awakening, the taking control of energies, a state of concentration that reinforces the strength of the initiate."[12]

Each of these states is seen as a level or degree of possession. Manifestation of spirit takes its recipient into one or other of these distinguishable states. *Nan dòmi,* the lucid dream state, is perhaps the most frequently perceived by outsiders or onlookers as the possession.

Dreaming While Awake:
Entry into the Realm of the Ancestors

Beaubrun learns from the highly developed consciousness of Aunt Tansia as well as her own experience about the initiation described as the entry into *anba dlo* "in the depths of the water, or in the mysteries of the water. Refers to a kind of initiation into the Ginen (i.e., African) mysteries."[13]

In many African religious traditions, the dead enter a universe parallel to the one in which the living exist, "close to our own—close enough to touch, though normally we cannot see it." This universe is a "vast reservoir of spiritual energy" that can be found "on the dark side of any mirror, or beneath the surface of any pool, and especially below the surface of the ocean, where we must find *Ginen anba dlo*—Africa beneath the waters. When slaves said that by drowning themselves in the ocean they would return to Africa, this is what they meant."[14]

Aunt Tansia explains to Beaubrun that the cult of the ancestors is the "key to all the magic of Vodou."[15] Beaubrun quotes her: "The cult of the ancestors holds the authority to lift up the veil of legends and of divination, the revelation of the inside and outside of things, the connections between the known world and the unknown world, the mysteries of the lwa open only to initiates."[16]

To be initiated into Haitian Vodou, then, and for that matter into many if not all African religious traditions, is to be ushered into and attain the conscious capacity to enter the parallel universe wherein the ancestors dwell. Initiation is an ushering into this level of consciousness. Aunt Tansia explains, "The cult of ancestors is a cult of possession. The initiate is the vehicle through which the ancestors transmit messages for the group. Thus, one must venerate and fear them. They are the elements that constitute the visible and the invisible worlds. They are the divine entities that constitute the Vodou pantheon. They participate in the existence of things. Through the trances of the initiate, they speak, sing, dance, listen to complaints, solve thorny problems, resolve difficulties, treat maladies, and reconcile the worst enemies."[17]

In the trance, or while possessed, or better still when one enters the elevated state of consciousness associated with the manifestation of spirit, one "sees" into the parallel universe of the ancestors and divine entities. "Seeing" says Beaubrun, "is being in a trance, and it brings joy."[18]

Beaubrun further explains:

The initiate, in the midst of his transformation, is in a state of complete beatitude. During the trance, he experiences a sense of wonder mixed with fear in view of the mysterious worlds he encounters. The initiate is an independent explorer of the universe. His voyages resemble dreams, but dreams experienced in a wakened state. To enter Nan Dòmi is to have the capacity to see what others do not perceive. The joy felt by the seer is a gentle emotion. It brings peace.[19]

Somatization of Spiritual Principles

The phenomenon long spoken of as "spirit possession" is therefore perhaps much better understood as an elevation of consciousness resulting from the manifestation of a spiritual entity such as a spirit or an ancestor. When spirit manifests in human experience, consciousness is raised to higher levels than the ordinary. People experience seeing, hearing, and moving in another realm. They see what others do not, hear what others do not, and move in ways that others normally are unable to. This is for them seeing, hearing, moving in other levels of consciousness. It is experiencing life in the unseen realm while living in the material realm. Adepts and others who have been similarly elevated recognize the entities manifesting through their characteristic manner of movement.

Associated with each *orisa* is a specific form of dance movement. Professor of Dance and Afro-American Studies Yvonne Daniel aptly articulates and lists various chants and movement sequences associated with the *orichas* Chango, Elegua, Ogun, Babaluayé, Yemayá, Ochun, Oya, and Orunmila across Haiti, Cuba, and Bahia, Brazil.[20] Daniel shows that the dancing body of participants in ritual and worship becomes a suprahuman body as the result of "spiritual transformation, when the worshipping, believing, and dancing human body is prepared for or overwhelmed by arrival of spiritual force." This human body "proceeds to unfold spiritual energy" and "to present or manifest divinities, who are aspects of a Supreme Divinity."[21] For, "the dancing body still functions within ritual communities as a source of spiritual communication, aesthetic expression, and the site of extraordinary transformations."[22]

In essence, then, what is happening in manifestation (possession) is an incarnation of the divine principles referred to as deities, gods, or goddesses. The possessed manifest these energies in their bodies. The principles become incarnated and express themselves in the movement and verbal expressions of the recipients.

African spiritual care in practice seeks to enhance and foster such incarnation and elevation of consciousness. Initiated African spiritual care practitioners have experienced such manifestations of spirit and are enabled to enter those states of consciousness as and when necessary. They are thereby enabled to diagnose the ailments of those around them who may consult them. They are also thereby given insight into the herbal, ritual, or ceremonial remedies that will result in the desired healing or guidance. African spiritual care is a result of an energized openness to, awareness of, and embodied engagement with this "unseen" dimension of existence.

Notes

1. Sheila S. Walker, *Ceremonial Spirit Possession in Africa and Afro-America* (E. J. Brill, 1972), 1.
2. Walker, *Ceremonial Spirit Possession*, 1.
3. Walker, *Ceremonial Spirit Possession*, 2.
4. The quotation is from Anthony F. C. Wallace, "Cultural Determinants of Responses to Hallucinatory Experience," *AMA Archives of General Psychiatry* no. 1 (1959), 59; cited in Sheila Walker, *Ceremonial Spirit Possession*, 3.
5. The reference is to John Beattie, *Other Cultures* (Free Press of Glencoe, 1964), 229, referred to in Walker, 3.
6. Mimerose P. Beaubrun, *Nan Dòmi: An Initiate's Journey into Haitian Vodou*, trans. D. J. Walker (City Lights, 2013), 27.
7. Beaubrun, *Nan Dòmi*, 31.
8. Beaubrun, *Nan Dòmi*, 178 (my underlining).
9. Beaubrun, *Nan Dòmi*, 175. The explanation of "poto mitan" can be found on 277.
10. Beaubrun, *Nan Dòmi*, 273–74.
11. Beaubrun *Nan Dòmi*, 276.
12. Beaubrun, *Nan Dòmi*, 277.
13. Beaubrun, *Nan Dòmi*, 271.
14. Beaubrun, *Nan Dòmi*, 15.
15. Beaubrun, *Nan Dòmi*, 222.
16. Beaubrun, *Nan Dòmi*, 222.
17. Beaubrun, *Nan Dòmi*, 223.
18. Beaubrun, *Nan Dòmi*, 227.

19. Beaubrun, *Nan Dòmi*, 227.
20. Yvonne Daniel, *Dancing Wisdom: Embodied Knowledge in Haitian Vodou, Cuban Yoruba, and Bahian Candomblé* (University of Illinois Press, 2005). See chapter 8.
21. Daniel, *Dancing Wisdom*, 61.
22. Daniel, *Dancing Wisdom*, 61.

4

Challenges to Life

Chaos, Evil, and Misfortune in African Religious Cultures

ONE OF THE MOST MISLEADING characterizations of African religion has been the depiction and naming of priests of this tradition by Western scholars and researchers as "witch doctors." The overarching implications of this naming are twofold. First, that the priests of African religion are themselves "witches" in the old European sense of typically female practitioners of evil who fly by night on broomsticks and do harm to innocent or unsuspecting people. Second, these priests major in destroying people's lives through manipulation of spiritual powers and working with others in the promotion of nefarious and destructive practices.

Christian and Islamic missionaries capitalized on and promoted these characterizations to give them advantages in the competition with African religious practitioners for the allegiance of potential members for their churches and faith communities. Priest-healers of African religion as such have the overwhelmingly unfortunate image in popular cultures of Africa and the rest of the world as charlatans, evil fraudsters, tricksters, wicked magicians, and manipulators.

Africans share in the common human quest for an understanding of the sources and causes of challenges to the well-being of all of creation. As in all other societies there are long-established ways of thinking about and responding to or treating specific ailments that befall humanity. In classic African thought, evil or misfortune can be said to be any experience that is injurious, painful, hurtful, regretful, or calamitous that impedes or obstructs the achievement of goals, ideals, happiness, or general well-being of individuals and communities.

Let us begin by examining the question of the sources of evil and misfortune.

Where Does Misfortune Come From?

From the perspective of classic African religious practitioners, misfortune, destruction to life or property, challenges to well-being, illness, tragedy, droughts, famine, and other such occurrences and circumstances originate from any or all of the three spheres of existence: (1) the unseen invisible or spiritual realm; (2) the human, personal, or social realm; and (3) the natural, material, physical or seen realm.

It is important from the outset to note that in classic African thought, plurality exists in all these realms. Put otherwise, there are many varied occupants, beings, or forces in each of the realms of existence.

The unseen realm is where the Creator, deities, ancestors, the dead, nature spirits, the yet-to-be-born, and other spiritual entities reside and operate from.

The seen realm can be subdivided into two dimensions—the human, (personal and social) and nature (physical, material world).

The *human* realm is where living human beings are, in all our varieties of life-state, including gender, ethnicity, class, social status, spiritual abilities, moral character, and so on.

The *natural* realm is where plants, herbs, rivers, trees, mountains, seas, minerals, material objects, and other naturally occurring phenomena exist.

Realms of Existence: Distinguishable but Inseparable

As previously noted, these three realms are distinguishable for purposes of understanding but are effectively inseparable. They are interconnected and as such influence or impact each other.

For instance, the natural and the human realms are deeply connected. Traditional African narratives are full of stories of how particular families are associated with specific animals, plants, rivers, or mountains. Whole communities may be categorized as belonging to or connected with specific animals, plants, or naturally occurring geographic features. These are typically described as *totems*. My own paternal people are understood to be connected to the ocean. We are ocean people. Thomas elaborates this point by saying "it was a taboo (sin) to kill certain animals or cut down sacred trees, which the people believed were endowed with the same life force as human beings. Various trees and plants were venerated and served a vital role in maintaining the ontological balance needed to prevent communal disasters."[1]

What happens in one realm has implications for and effects on others. As will be discussed further in chapter 6, life and well-being of individuals and communities is intricately and integrally linked to harmony between and within the realms. It is *conflict between realms that is the ultimate source of misfortune.*

Inter-Realm Conflict: The Ultimate Source of Trouble

The notion that conflict or disharmony between the realms is ultimately the source of all misfortune fuels a great deal of spiritual care work from a classic African viewpoint.

Thomas, in presenting this insight, makes the following ecologically significant point.

Practitioners of traditional African cultural forms do not view themselves at odds with the natural world. Nor do they struggle to tame or dominate the environment because human beings are an integral part of nature. Traditional Africans have never viewed themselves as being at war with nature but instead seek to become one with it. Those who are disconnected from nature are in essence at war with themselves. Those who pollute the environment for material gain are waging a senseless war against themselves. Nature will expel them from the earth before they are successful at destroying Mother Earth.[2]

Because Africans classically view themselves as part and parcel of nature, to be disconnected from nature or to desecrate nature is essentially a declaration of war against oneself and one's own existence. Destruction of nature is destruction of humanity.

In classic African thought, therefore, one of the cardinal goals of spiritual practice is the strengthening of the communion and harmony between the realms. Much of African ritual spiritual care activity is devoted to this. We are a part of nature, and in spiritual care we seek communion with nature.

African mystic Brother Ishmael Tetteh reminds us all of this with these words:, "We are beings of Nature brought here by Nature, which existed long before us and prepared itself to accommodate us."[3] Our truest spirituality therefore lies in our learning from the "sacred scriptures" of nature and living in harmony with it.

Causes of Misfortune Resulting from Inter-Realm Conflict

Explicit reference is made to the following occupants of the different realms of existence as the direct and immediate sources of trouble, chaos, and misfortune within community. Five notable identifiable sources of chaos are the following.

First are *the troubled dead*. Examples of the dead who are in a troubled and unrestful state are murdered people whose lives were unceremoniously cut short. Others are people whose death was not marked by the requisite funerary and burial rites or rituals. Such can and do foment troubles for the living such as social disharmony, chaos, or confusion in national life, as well as natural disasters such as floods and famines.

Second are *ancestors and deities who have been neglected* or disregarded. Those who have lived well and made contributions to the human communities they were a part of while living are accorded the status of ancestors in death. They are commemorated and memorialized after death and are believed to act on behalf of the living. Where such people, as well as deities or divinities, go unattended or are neglected, they are believed to cause suffering within human communities.

Third, some spiritual entities are regarded as being willfully troublesome or by nature *malevolent spirits or forces*. These spiritual beings by nature are troublemakers. They are invoked to bring about the overthrow of evil regimes, the punishment of criminals, or the destruction of unwanted institutions.

Fourth, evil can emanate entirely from *the human community* with no immediate influence from the unseen realm. Where there is hatred, jealousy, or hostility among people within particular or else different communities, misfortunes of various kinds can result.

Fifth, *human wrongdoing*, typically of a relational nature, can result in misfortunes. Since every human person is understood to be a composite of different aspects—such as okra, sunsum, mogya (Akan), chi (Igbo)—personal (internal) disharmony or conflicts between these different facets of personality can also result in misfortunes such as physical illness.

How Is Evil Transmitted or Conveyed?

Having identified the sources or causative agents of misfortune, let us now discuss the question of the means by which they are believed to cause havoc. In classic African thought the animating force flowing through all of life is described using various terminologies. At core this is understood to be spiritual in nature. Various terms such as *vital-life force, psychic power,* or *mystic energy* are used for this spiritual energy seen as the animating force of existence.

Adama and Naomi Doumbia use the Mande term *nyama* for it and define it as follows. "Nyama: the energy of Spirit that flows throughout the universe. It is the life force that links everything together"[4]

Declares a traditional African priest/healer,

Nyama is the energy that emanates from Spirit and flows throughout the universe. It is the life force that links all of existence together, humans, animals, plants, and minerals. The power of creation and destruction, nyama commands everything from bountiful harvests to droughts and plagues; it directs the twinkling stars and the rippling tides. The energy of the universe shapes nature into its many forms and yields to our handling of its power. We draw life from this potent force that connects all of creation. It is the fuel for all our activities. Nyama is the source of energy for every word, thought, and action. To live harmoniously with nature, we live with a sensitivity to the power of nyama. To recognize this energy is to appreciate that everything is interconnected, integral parts of a whole.

Classic African practitioners make clear that the issue at stake with relation to this life force is the power of knowledge:

Those of us with high levels of nyama, such as shamans, diviners, blacksmiths, bards, and hunters, can maneuver this energy and direct it at will. The ability to channel nyama requires access to advanced levels of mystical knowledge. Those who possess this knowledge hold great influence in our communities. One may devote limitless time and effort to learn how to direct this energy, but most of us leave it to our artisans who inherit large concentrations of nyama from their ancestors. One must also learn to handle nyama through intensive training, as it can be deadly if one does not follow the appropriate rituals for engaging it. Our artisans spend their entire lives cultivating their relationship with this power.[5]

Along similar lines, Magesa argues that there are three essential characteristics of classic African life and thought. First, "all existence consists of energy or power." In other words, it consists of active, existential forces that continually and consistently interact with and influence one another (for good or evil).[6] Second, "all creatures participate in the comprehensive power of life, each to a different degree, at their own level within the whole."[7] Third, "all vital energies existing in the universe, that is, the spirit of existence, coalesce to serve human life."[8]

Spiritual Energy Is Neutral

What is abundantly clear in the discourse of African practitioners is that the spiritual energy they have access to, like electricity, is *neutral*. Like a sharp knife it can be utilized for beneficial as well as destructive purposes.

In his classic study of African religions and philosophy Professor John Mbiti writes: "Mystical power is neither good nor evil in itself: but when used maliciously by some individuals, it is experienced as evil. This view makes evil an independent and external object which, however, cannot act on its own but must be employed by human or spiritual agents."[9] Practitioners and adepts of classic African religion repeatedly assert that all genuine priest-healers of African religion undergo training that emphasizes the importance of an ethically worthy utilization of spiritual energy. This is a cardinal principle in the ethics of the practice of spiritual care within the classic guilds of African religious practice.[10]

Nevertheless, the discussion of evil and harming within African social and religious contexts would be incomplete without a careful, although necessarily brief, consideration of the destructive phenomena pervasively referred to on the African continent and beyond it as "witchcraft."

Witchcraft

Witchcraft in this sense is a generic term for all that is evil, destructive, harmful, opposed to human flourishing, and generally anti-life in purpose and practice. It is an intolerable contradiction of the values of life and community that are held in high esteem among African communities worldwide.

Zimbabwean social anthropologist and professor Munyaradzi Mawere explains, "A common notion underlying witchcraft is the metaphysical belief that supernatural forces may be used as a means to achieve certain complicated indigenous knowledges/epistemologies and personal goals which include harm, profit and fertility." Mawere defines witchcraft as "a practice that involves the use of potentially harmful medicines, charms, magic and any other supernatural means or devices to cause some positive effects (such as wealth accumulation, social power) or negative consequences (such as psychological or physical harm, illness, misfortune or death of other people, animals or property)." Mawere, like many traditionalists, recognizes that "supernatural" power or energy can be employed for beneficial as well as harmful purposes. Thus, in African life and thought, witchcraft does represent the ability to harness the forces of life to effect clear ends.

Mawere explains further, "this is because witchcraft beliefs embrace a wide range of ideas, beliefs, practices, and motivations, but in their various forms they usually share the idea that the power to inflict injury and benefit could be exercised through unobservable supernatural means. Witches and wizards—those involved in the practice of witchcraft—are thought to possess extraordinary powers that enable them to perform ritual practices and act beyond the capabilities of ordinary human beings."[11]

For some African people such powers are understood to be an inherited propensity passed down generationally. An individual who possesses such power to a high degree may be unconscious of having it. In such cases its employment to destructive ends may be compulsive, with the practitioner unable to resist its usage. In other cases, individuals are fully conscious of it, having intentionally acquired it in exchange for money, material goods, or animal or human lifeblood.

Africans understand that by choice humans can and do employ spiritual energy for nefarious purposes. Such evil is a reality against which people of goodwill must contend. Practitioners of spiritual care must be aware of this power and know how to work effectively against its harmful use. They must, of necessity, also know how to unleash the beneficial effects of spiritual energy.

Notions of Evil

The discussion of "evil," "sin," or "destructiveness" in African religious discourse is characterized by at least four major conceptual frames.

First, a concept of "Satan" as the personal embodiment of absolute evil is not present in many precolonial classic African religious cultures. An example of this can be found in Igbo culture.[12] Nigerian philosopher and scholar of religion Ejikemeuwa Ndubisi argues, in my view correctly, that "the western concept of 'Satan' as the arch-enemy of God and the supreme author of evil, whose one purpose is to frustrate the goodness of God and to disseminate evil, who takes delight in inciting men to moral evil so as to alienate them from Him, does not exist in Igbo religion."[13] As with early Judaism, in African thought, the Great Deity or Supreme Being is the ultimate source of all, good and evil.

Second, many "trickster/teacher-examiner" deities exist in African myths and narratives. Examples of these include Ananse (the spider entity of Akan mythology) and the Yoruba deity Eshu Elegba, perhaps best characterized as "master of paradox." As with the Igbo deity of war, Ekwensu, these examiner-trickster deities have erroneously been translated as the Satan of Christian and Islamic discourse.

Third, wrongdoing, or sin, is generally seen as acts or omissions committed against the *sensus communis* (community). Wrongdoing is egregious, not so much because it represents a moral failing of an individual person but because it infringes on a communal relational reality. Sin, in classic African thought, essentially transgresses human relationality in community.

Fourth, evil can and must be ritually cleansed and atoned for. Rituals, including sacred offerings, spiritual herbal baths, and sacrifices, are performed to mitigate the consequences and effects of evil. In this regard African priest-healers receive as a crucial part of their training within the sacred shrines the knowledge and expertise in what may be described as "spiritual technologies" that bring well-being to people. Codes of practice for such priests include the "do no harm" of Hippocratic oath, except in the service of policing communities, protecting persons from the evil of malicious persons, or else as a means of punishing wrongdoers. African priest-healers learn how to neutralize, counteract, or reverse the harmful spiritual forces that evil persons may have unleashed in their desire to harm persons in their communities. Spiritual care in such instances takes the form of countering, negating, neutralizing, or redirecting negative forces away from their intended targets.

Order and Chaos in Ancient African Thought

Ancient Egyptian thought approached the questions of good and evil through postulating two *neters* or deities, namely Ma'at and *isfet*. The Egyptian term "neter," like the Yoruba word Orisha, is used in religious terms to refer to gods, goddesses, or spiritual entities. The same terms also mean "force of nature" or "life principle."

Ma'at is the principle of *order and balance* in the cosmos, the force of structure, meaning, truth, justice, reciprocity, virtue, health, propriety, and harmony. Ma'at was personified as a goddess, the daughter of the Sun Deity, Ra, and was associated with Djehuti (or Thoth), the neter of wisdom and communication. Ma'at had been present since the first stirring of the creation of the cosmos out of the formless waters of chaos. Once the cosmos had fully come into existence, she was charged with upholding it and preventing it from slipping back into formlessness. Ma'at was closely associated with Ra, the highest neter or god and original pharaoh of the gods of Egypt, as his wife or daughter. During Ra's daily circle around the sky, Ma'at accompanied and guarded him, ensuring that this journey, essential as it was to the well-being of the cosmos on all levels, went as it should. There were, after all, agents of chaos lurking on his flanks, trying to devour him or knock him off course. This role of ma'at in human life therefore created a continuity between religion, political action, ethics, and morality.

Ma'at, in ancient African thought, stands in opposition to *disorder and chaos* or *isfet*, which essentially means "lack" (lack of meaning, lack of order, lack of form) that manifests in sickness, death, scarcity, injustice, falsehood, theft, violence, war, and enmity.

The concept of ma'at (order, goodness) was fundamental in Egyptian ethical and moral thought. The king's role was to establish ma'at in place of isfet (disorder). Ma'at was crucial in human life and embraced notions of reciprocity, justice, truth, and moderation.

In its abstract sense, ma'at was the divine order established at creation and reaffirmed at the accession of each new king of Egypt. In setting ma'at in place of isfet, the king played the role of the sun god, the god with the closest links to ma'at. Ma'at stood at the head of the sun god's bark as it traveled through the sky and the underworld. Although aspects of kingship and of ma'at were at times subjected to criticism and reformulation, the principles underlying these two institutions were fundamental to ancient Egyptian life and thought.

Professor Maulana Karenga presents perhaps the most scholarly study of ma'at in *The Moral Ideal in Ancient Egypt*. He writes, "in its essential meaning, *Maat is rightness in the spiritual and moral sense in three realms: the Divine, the natural and the social.* In its expansive sense, *Maat is an interrelated order of rightness which requires and is the result of right relations with and right behavior towards the Divine, nature and other humans.*"[14]

Conclusion

In classic African religious thought, then, beneficence as well as maleficence exist and flow forth from the realms of existence, both unseen and seen. The realm of spirits, the divine realm as well as the earth plane, is populated by entities possessed of this dual nature, capable of bringing forth and spreading goodness or chaos, blessing or destruction. No participant in any of the realms is "all good" or "all bad." All of creation, like all divine existence, is a mixture of order and chaos. Within each spiritual entity, as in nature, there is the capacity to do great good as well as to be harmful and destructive. Both abilities are employable in the exercise of the entity's function. The supreme task of living is managing and balancing this reality so that beneficence for the entire community prevails over maleficence. This essentially is the attitude and orientation of classic African religious life and thought and underlies the functions of spiritual care practitioners within African life.

African spiritual care ultimately serves the purpose of establishing ma'at in the human community. African spiritual care practitioners are at work promoting and facilitating the well-being and flourishing of all existence, and the control or expulsion of the chaotic or destructive forces that equally exist in creation.

Notes

1. Douglas E. Thomas, *African Traditional Religion in the Modern World* (McFarland, 2013), 183.
2. Thomas, *African Traditional Religion*, 182.
3. Ishmael Tetteh, *New Era of Spirituality: Spirituality from the Wisdom of Nature* (Conscious Humanity Press, 2021), 25.

4. Adama Doumbia and Naomi Doumbia, eds., *The Way of the Elders: West African Spirituality & Tradition* (Llewellyn, 2004), 167.

5. Doumbia and Doumbia, *The Way of the Elders*, 5.

6. Laurenti Magesa, *What Is Not Sacred? African Spirituality* (Orbis, 2013), 33.

7. Magesa, *What Is Not Sacred?*, 33.

8. Magesa, *What Is Not Sacred?*, 33.

9. John S. Mbiti, *African Religions and Philosophy* (Heinemann, 1969), 27.

10. See, for example, the Code of Ethics of the African National Healers Association: https://www.africannationalhealersassociation.org/code-of-ethics

11. Munyaradzi Mawere, *African Belief and Knowledge Systems* (Langaa Research & Publishing Common Initiative Group, 2011), 92.

12. See E. J. O. Ndubisi, "The Notion of Satan/Ekwensu: A Comparative Study of Western and African (Igbo) Thoughts," *OWIJOPPA* 3, no. 1 (2019), 2630–7057, 23–36. He argues convincingly that the Igbo deity of war Ekwensu is wrongly translated by Western Christians as the "Satan" of Western Christian formulation.

13. Ndubisi, "The Notion of Satan/Ekwensu," 34.

14. Maulana Karenga, *Maat: The Moral Ideal in Ancient Egypt: A Study in Classical African Ethics* (Routledge, 2004), 10.

5

Divination and Divine Guidance

I N CLASSIC AFRICAN RELIGION PRACTICES that have been termed "divination" by Western scholars are basically rituals engaged in to seek guidance from the parallel universe (the unseen world) where ancestors, spirits, and deities reside. These rituals are understood to be the language of the unseen world. They are thus understood to be the most powerful means of communicating with that realm in quest of responses from there that are deemed to be helpful in dealing with issues of life in this seen realm. Divinatory practices are engaged as a means of communicating with the ancestors, deities, and spirits of the unseen realm. Divinatory rituals teach practitioners the languages of the unseen realm through spiritual disciplines such as libation, prayer, fasting, abstinence, and discernment. Such disciplines heighten people's abilities to "see," "hear," and "perceive" responses or directives from that unseen realm.

Adama and Naomi Doumbia explain that "our diviners enable us to communicate with the realm of the spirits and with our ancestors, to determine whether or not we are on our correct spiritual paths and fulfilling our true destinies."[1]

As discussed in chapter 3, initiation into Haitian vodou or other forms of African religion opens the mind, elevates the level of consciousness, and facilitates the perceptive powers of an initiate, enabling them to "divine," which often entails predicting the future; having insight into present, often secret or hidden, realities; and prescribing forms of ritual or spiritual activities that can reverse negative circumstances or facilitate healing and well-being.

The late great Dagara medicine man, diviner, and philosopher Malidoma Patrice Somé details his initiation into the depths of Dagara religious practice in his compelling autobiographical work, *Of Water and the Spirit: Ritual, Magic, and Initiation in the Life of an African Shaman.*[2] The late South African Zulu traditional healer, diviner, sculptor, painter, and master teacher Vusamazulu Credo Mutwa similarly gives his own first-hand accounts and personal experiences as a *sangoma* (Zulu shaman) in his book *Zulu Shaman: Dreams, Prophecies, and Mysteries.*[3] Professor Marta Moreno Vega recounts the fascinating story of her own journey from ignorance and skepticism to initiation as a Yoruba priestess in the Santeria religion in *The Altar of My Soul: The Living Traditions of Santería.*[4] These three, all of whom are highly qualified academic scholars trained in the West, all became practitioners and diviners within their African religious traditions. Their books give firsthand insider perspectives of the divinatory practices of classic African religion.

Divination: Systematic Processes of Seeking Direction

Divination in classic African religion is a systematic and carefully crafted process of connecting with the unseen world and seeking and receiving direction for living in this world. Philip Peek, in one of the most far-reaching anthropological studies of African divinatory work, offers this definition of a divination system: "A divination system is a standardized process deriving from a learned discipline based on an extensive body of knowledge. This knowledge may or may not be literally expressed during the interpretation of the oracular message. The diviner may utilize a fixed corpus, such as the Yoruba Ifa Odu verses, or a more diffuse body of esoteric knowledge."[5] It is important to stress the "standardized process" in Peek's characterization. Classic African diviners are not haphazard in their activities but rather follow carefully established disciplines and procedures. These are based on bodies of knowledge that are studied in sacred shrines or through extensive practical experience.

There are many different divining processes, but all follow laid-down routines that facilitate the obtaining of information that would otherwise be inaccessible. The routine or ritual process is akin to the correct articulation of words in a language that conveys to a listener who understands that language the requests and intentions of a speaker. Ritual unlocks the meaning and significance of what is happening and makes possible both comprehension and relevant responses to it.

African diviners typically use devices such as cowrie shells, calabashes holding water into which special herbs or plants have been placed, kola nuts, beads, earth, sand, flowers, fruits, leaves, stems, barks, roots, seeds, and eggs, to name a few. Through "spirit possession" or, as discussed in the previous chapter, better termed "the manifestation of a spirit or deity," the diviner's body may itself become the vehicle or device through which the knowledge is communicated. In this cross-realm communication, ancestors or spirit entities inhabiting the unseen world speak through the diviner.

Adama and Naomi Doumbia write about recipes in their own divining and healing work: "We possess countless recipes and instructions for the use of these materials to accomplish almost any goal or activity. Our recipes enable us to treat all kinds of illnesses and ailments. We also keep instructions for the creation of any kind of charm, which can bring protection, success, and anything one desires."[6] They go on to explain that it is the proper and wise use of the recipes that distinguishes between a true healer and "an individual who may use these recipes to harm others or to gain material things at the expense of others."[7]

It is critical to stress that African divination systems are multisensory and variously utilize all forms of communication. It is understood that the other world "speaks" through otherwise inanimate divinatory objects, such as marked tablets, half-shells on a string, or objects in a diviner's basket.

In some divinatory systems the answers from the unseen realm are revealed clearly and plainly to all in the consultation or gathering. In others, such as in the casting of cowrie shells, the response must be interpreted by the diviner. This is the case with the readings or divinations in the Yoruba Ifa system, which are interpreted through the elaborate literature of the Odus.

Divining as Ethical Practice: Cross-Realm Relations and Communication

In most African societies it is held that living persons must maintain proper relations with the spiritual entities such as ancestors inhabiting the unseen realm in order to live a good life. For diviners this is even more critical. The special relationship and rapport necessary between diviner and spirit—and that between diviner and client—is at times expressed in terms of twinning; that is, the diviner and spirit establish a relationship as if they are twins. From her research with the Djimini Senufo of Côte d'Ivoire, Ellen Suthers pursues the twinning metaphor in the following interpretation:

> Sharing the same womb experience, twins become endowed with, or constituted of, the same perceptions; hence they emerge in the world having congruent images. Because they share perfect knowledge and perceptions of each other and of the spirit realm, twins do not need speech to communicate with each

other or with the host of spiritual entities. . . . As pairing makes the client congruent with the diviner and the diviner congruent with the spirits, all come to share a common perception. Through gestures, the diviner transforms his or her body to reflect the image of the client, and thus to reveal the client's problem in concrete terms.[8]

Another example of this can be found among the Baule of Côte d'Ivoire, West Africa, where diviners' home shrines always include pairs of spirit figures that assist them in their work. These images depict two figures back-to-back in a Janus pose, or one on the shoulders of another, as if to portray the merging of diviner and spirit. Indeed, most African diviners work with a variety of spirit "helpers" who "manifest in" the diviner during divination sessions to provide oracular messages.

These descriptions express the critical dynamics of divination in many African cultures. The crucial relationality between the human person (diviner, healer, priest/healer) and the unseen realm (spiritual entities, ancestors, divine beings) is what is noteworthy in this. At stake in these processes that operate whether through diviners or through their devices are the relationship and communication between realms.

Designing and Performing

African divination rituals typically end with a final diagnosis and the devising of an action plan. It is noteworthy that these aspects of the process clearly highlight the communal nature of the entire process. The diviner who has been in close interaction with the spiritual entities, and in empathic attunement with the client(s), has thereby become an intermediary between persons and realms of existence. As human representative of the client, they have ritually communicated the questions and desires of the clients to the unseen realm. As spokesperson of the gods, they bring messages and directions from the spiritual realm to the humans seeking guidance. What remains is how the direction received will be implemented in the lives of the clients. For this, consultation and discussion are paramount, and the clients and diviners typically work this out, including consideration of any alternative lines of action that are practicable and no less effective as remedies.

Conclusion

Divination in classic African religion, then, is a means, par excellence, of communication between the realms of existence. It is an avenue by which humans seek and obtain divine and ancestral guidance from those with much more experience and knowledge than the living. Ritual is the language of the heavenly unseen realm and is thus the means of communication employed in this endeavor. The divine realm is where creation emanated from. The originators and creators of this earth most definitely have more knowledge of the workings of this life than the present inhabitants. The ancestors have lived and successfully navigated this earth's realm. They necessarily have more experience and can offer much better guidance as to how to navigate life's exigencies than living humans. Through divination this vast reservoir of knowledge and experience is tapped for the betterment and upliftment of humanity.

Notes

1. Adama Doumbia and Naomi Doumbia, eds., *The Way of the Elders: West African Spirituality & Tradition* (Llewellyn, 2004), 26.

2. Malidoma Patrice Somé, *Of Water and the Spirit* (Penguin, 1994).

3. Vusamazulu Credo Mutwa, *Zulu Shaman: Dreams, Prophecies, and Mysteries* (Destiny, 2003).

4. Marta Moreno Vega, *The Altar of My Soul: The Living Traditions of Santeria* (Ballantine, 2000).

5. Philip M. Peek, ed., *African Divination Systems* (Indiana University Press, 1991), 2.

6. Doumbia and Doumbia, *The Way of the Elders*, 31.

7. Doumbia and Doumbia, *The Way of the Elders*, 31.

8. Ellen Suthers, "Perception, Knowledge and Divination in Djimini Society, Ivory Coast" (Unpublished PhD diss., University of Virginia, 1987), 11–12, 16.

6

Health, Healing, and Wholeness

IN A HISTORICAL NOVEL SET in late nineteenth-century Africa, African writer and professor of English Literature Ayi Kwei Armah captures the work and words of African traditional healers. Though fictional, *The Healers* portrays the ideals and the practices of Africa's classic spiritual care providers. In a central portion of the book, traditional healer Damfo[1] is being questioned by a young inquirer, Densu:[2]

> "What really is a healer's work?" Densu asked
> "You may say it's seeing. And hearing. Knowing."
> "I don't understand," Densu told Damfo.
> "Take any place, the forest, say. Men walk through the forest. They see leaves, trees, insects, sometimes a small animal, perhaps a snake. They see many things. But they see little. They hear many forest sounds. But they hear little."
> "A healer sees more?" Densu asked.
> "A healer sees differently. He hears differently," Damfo answered. "Yes, he hears and sees more."

As observed earlier in our discussion of spirit manifestation, it is precisely this ability to "see" more intensely and comprehensively, and to "hear" more fully and expansively that mark the spiritual care provider in classic African thought. The healer continues:

Say a snake bites a child. Those who walk through the forest with their ordinary eyes see the child near death, lying there helpless in the middle of all the leaves of the forest. The healer sees not just a mass of leaves. He can recognize the different spirit in each kind of leaf. He can see the leaf that has a spirit opposite to, and stronger than, the snake's poison. He can squeeze out its juice for the spirit contained in it and use it to save the child. You see, it is as if the spirits of all the leaves of the forest were talking to the healer, telling him what it is they each contain, what it is each can do, and what they cannot do. The leaves, animals, even stones, say much, and they show much, to any prepared to see and hear.

The discussion continues with Densu asking, "Why can't others see and hear?"

> "They could if they prepared themselves to see and
>   hear."
> "Can't people see and hear naturally?"
> "What do you mean, naturally?" the healer asked the
>   boy.
> "Without preparation."
> "No one sees without preparation. Not the healer's
>   kind of seeing."
> "Yet you made seeing sound very natural."
> "It is," agreed the healer. "And preparation isn't
>   unnatural. It is also natural."
> "But children, no one prepares them to see anything."
> "Adults do that," the healer said. "A child has eyes for
>   seeing light and shade and color. But seeing for
>   ordinary people isn't just that, is it? It's knowing
>   what the light and shade and color go to make.
>   Recognition is what people call seeing. What
>   healers mean by seeing isn't just that."
> "Is hearing the same?"

> "More so. The ear hears the sound. When a child
>   understands language, he hears more than sound.
>   The meaning is in the arrangement of sounds."

Much as the gifts of traditional medicine are received by divine gifting, so is there training and preparation that are given under the tutelage of experienced priests. Armah's narrative continues:

> "What is the healer's preparation for hearing and
>   seeing?"
> "The answer is a matter of years. Three years to start
>   with. But in truth the preparation is endless."
> "Does a healer know languages others don't know?"
> "You want to understand it that way. You know how
>   full of sounds the world is. Some of these sounds
>   we are taught to understand. Most we don't
>   understand, ever. In the universe there are so many
>   signs. A few we understand, the way farmers know
>   what clouds mean, and fishermen understand stars.
>   But most signs mean nothing to us because we
>   aren't prepared to understand them. The healer
>   trains his eye—so he can read signs. His training is
>   of the ears—so he can listen to sounds and
>   understand them. His preparation is also of the
>   nostrils—life and death have their smells. It is of
>   the tongue, the body's ability to feel."

Damfo articulates most clearly and powerfully the outcome of shrine training for all African traditional medicine-people:

> After his training the healer walks through the same world
> every person walks through. But he sees signs others don't see.
> He hears sounds others don't hear. The same tree that just
> stands there dumbly to everyone, to the healer its leaves have
> things to say. The healer learns the meaning of the river's
> sound, of the sounds of the forest animals. And when he needs

the curing spirit from a plant, if his eyes are well prepared, he may see from a great distance some small sign of the leaf that is ready to be taken.

African Medicine: A Matter of Moral Character

The conversation gains in intensity and purpose when the young inquirer begins to ask more specifically about the nature of healer and the craft of healing.

> "Can everyone become a healer?" asks young Densu.
> "Few ever want to be healers."
> "But could everyone be a healer?"
> "No."
> "Why not?"
> "The healer must first have a healer's nature."
> "What is that?"
> "I can't tell you what it is, just so," said Damfo. "But for a beginning, he who would be a healer must set great value on seeing truly, hearing truly, understanding truly, and acting truly." The healer laughed at himself. "You see why healing can't be a popular vocation? The healer would rather see and hear and understand than have power over men. Most people would rather have power over men than see and hear."
> "What gives the healer his nature?"
> "The same that gives him life."
> "What is that?"
> "I do not know," the healer said. Densu looked at his face and knew he was telling the truth.
> "You said for a beginning."
> "Yes," Damfo said. "It's not enough for the one who would be a healer to have a healer's nature. Beyond that he needs training, preparation."
> "Is it hard?"

"Infinitely so."

"What does it consist of?"

"We don't talk about it just to talk," said Damfo
evenly. "The only people who need to discuss a
healer's training are those actually undergoing it."

"What makes it so hard?"

"Many things. For one thing, the healer devotes
himself to inspiration. He also lives against
manipulation."

"I think I understand inspiration," Densu said. "But
manipulation?"

"It's a disease, a popular one. If I'm not spiritually
blind, I see your spirit. I talk to it if I want to
invite you to do something with me. If your spirit
agrees it moves your body and your body acts.
That's inspiration. But if I'm blind to your spirit I
see only your body. Then if I want you to do
something for me I force or trick your body into
doing it even against your spirit's direction. That's
manipulation. Manipulation steals a person's
body from his spirit, cuts the body off from its
own spirit's direction. The healer is a lifelong
enemy of manipulation. The healer's method is
inspiration."

Healing Work Is Communal Work

African sacred healers see their work as transcending individual
well-being.

"We heal people, individuals. That's part of our work.
But it isn't all. It isn't even the greater part of it.
It's just a part. The whole of it concerns . . ." the
effort to find a word threatened to exasperate him,
but he breathed deep, smiled, and said with an air
of giving up ". . . wholeness. Those who learn to

read the signs around them and to hear the language of the universe reach a kind of knowledge healer's call the shadow. The shadow, because that kind of knowledge follows you everywhere. When you find it, it is not difficult at all. It says there are two forces, unity and division. The first creates. The second destroys; it's a disease, disintegration.

"It is the first, unity, that gives healing work its strength. Think of it. *Healing an individual person—what is that but restoring a lost unity to that individual's body and spirit?*

"*A people can be diseased the same way. Those who need naturally to be together but are not, are they not a people sicker than the individual body disintegrated from its soul? Sometimes a whole people needs healing work. Not a tribe, not a nation. Tribes and nations are just signs that the whole is diseased. The healing work that cures a whole people is the highest work, far higher that the cure of single individuals.*"

"Are health and unity the same, then?"

"To healers, yes," Damfo said. "There's health when everything that should work together works together. Take the single person. If body and soul are working together the mind thinks: I should do this; the will decides: I will do it; the muscle tenses itself to help the will: and the hand does what the mind has thought. Everything works together. But say there is a bone broken in the body. The mind may think something; the will may desire it; but when the muscle tries to move the hand, there are two pieces of the broken bone pushing against each other, fighting each other, instead of working together. That is disease. The

cure of that kind of disease is one of the first steps
in healing."

"Only the first steps?"

"Only one of the first steps. There is disease which
comes from conflict between body and soul in the
same individual. That is more serious and takes
much longer to cure. Years, usually."

"That is high work," Densu said.

"Not the highest though," the healer said. "There are
worse diseases needing healing. When one person
in a community—body and soul—clashes with
another individual in the same community that too
is disease."

"But is that also work for healers?"

*"The ending of all unnatural rifts is healing work.
When different groups within what should be a
natural community clash against each other, that
also is disease. That is why healers say that our
people, the way we are divided into petty nations,
are suffering from a terrible disease."*[3]

The quest for health and wellness is in African societies central to the functioning of religion and spiritual care. In a recent
comprehensive study of the place, role, and continuing significance of African healing shrines, Dr. Matthew Michael of
Nasarawa State University, Keffi, Nigeria, and historian
Professor Umar H. D. Danfulani of the University of Jos,
Nigeria, identified three cultural factors that drive the African
pursuit of wellness. First is the "grounding of African understanding of wellness in an ethno-cultural epistemology which
often subconsciously places spiritual knowledge over empirical
and scientific data."[4] This is not to say that Africans do not acknowledge and utilize empirical and scientific knowledge in their
quest for health. Rather, it affirms a social fact that is evident to
all health care practitioners throughout Africa, that "African

people in most of their quest for wellness privilege ethno-cultural modes of epistemologies rather than scientific ones."[5]

Second, "African shrines are cultural sites of ethnopsychology of the African people."[6] The researchers explain the term "ethnopsychology" as referring to a culturally grounded view of psychological phenomena that seeks to understand the individual and collective orientations of people from the inner workings of their worldviews. They point out another glaring social and religious fact evident across Africa as they refer to the fact that despite much stigmatization and demonization of African healing shrines by the mainstream monotheistic faiths of Christianity and Islam on the continent, "in the crisis of faith, most converts of Christianity and Islam have often consulted African healing shrines for their wellbeing, desired healing and guidance."[7]

There is a vast literature pointing to the fact that African Christianity and Islam have been influenced and often shaped by the ethnopsychological dynamisms of African healing shrines.[8] Michael and Danfulani state the observable when they assert, "African ethnopsychology is often glaring[ly] seen in the contemporary ministries of African Pentecostalism, African Independent churches and the creative operations of African Islamic medicine which is often the direct fusions of Islam, Arabic mysticism and traditional African Spirituality."[9]

The third cultural factor concerns herbal medicine. "African healing shrines are important sites in [the] African quest for wellness in its unique experimentation in ethnopharmacopeia, locally sourced remedies, and multidimensional perspectives."[10] Scientific studies increasingly establish the efficacy of some herbal remedies employed by African healers in the treatment of certain illnesses.[11] As with most pharmacological treatments, of course, debates continue.[12] Herbal treatments continue to be the most popular form of traditional medicine in Africa, and WHO reports that 70 percent to 80 percent of people in Africa have used a form of traditional medicine as primary health care. Herbal treatments are readily available and much more affordable for local African peoples than Western medicines tend to be. There is little doubt that healing and health care are central planks of spiritual care in African societies.

Let us now examine the first of the identified factors driving African's quest for wellness, namely an "ethnocultural epistemology."

African Ethnocultural Epistemologies

Traditional Medicine

The World Health Organization defines traditional medicine in general in the following way: "It is the sum total of the knowledge, skill, and practices based on the theories, beliefs, and experiences indigenous to different cultures, whether explicable or not, used in the maintenance of health as well as in the prevention, diagnosis, improvement or treatment of physical and mental illness."[13] Drs. Ampofo and Johnson-Romauld, in a discussion paper on traditional African medicine's role in the development of health care services in Africa published in 1978, drawing on this more general characterization, defined African traditional medicine as "The totality of all knowledge and practices, whether explicable or not, used in diagnosing, preventing, or eliminating a physical, mental or social disequilibrium and which rely exclusively on experience and observation handed down from generation to generation, verbally or in writing."[14] In both definitions the foundational role of traditional knowledge is affirmed. How, then, according to classic African thought, is this knowledge acquired? As Thomas argues, African "traditional healers hold that all sickness has an origin that must first be addressed before any attempts are made to treat outward manifestations that fail to address the root cause of a disease."[15]

What emerges from studies of African traditional healers and shrine priests and priestesses is that the principal pathways to knowledge are the following: (1) observation of nature, (2) insight, (3) revelation, (4) ritual, (5) symbol, and (6) rhythm and movement.

Observation of Nature

Repeatedly, African priest-healers have told me that their fore-parents and traditional professional predecessors observed the behavior of animals in their compounds and natural habitat when they were suffering particular ailments. Healers would observe what herbs or plants the animals would go to and how they would either lick, suck, chew, or else rub their own bodies on the trunks or barks of trees, shrubs, or bushes. These herbs or plants are then noted as potentially suitable human treatment for the kinds of symptoms the animal manifested. They are then employed on an experimental basis with their clients. This natural observation and experimentation, akin to the scientific method exercised in Western experimental science, is paramount in African healing arts. Traditional healers study these verbal and in certain cases written records, or else they are taught them by their mentors in the healing shrines where they train.

Insight

Cultivating an inner disposition of listening and hearing is one of the cardinal disciplines that trainee priest-healers undergo during their years of training in the shrines to which they have been led by the manifesting spiritual entity that summons them to this vocation. Knowledge, especially in diagnosis and treatment of illness, comes as insight to the traditional healer through meditation, prayer, or divining. The belief is that the unseen world of ancestors and spiritual entities with its superior knowledge of terrestrial matters also possesses the strong inclination to make that knowledge known on earth. The only problem is humanity's reluctance to engage the unseen world due to a pre-occupation with the allurements of the seen world. Vocation to priesthood, which will be discussed more fully in this chapter, is necessarily a calling to develop "inner ears and eyes" able to receive and interpret messages from that parallel universe.

Revelation

Revelation, another major way in which knowledge is received, takes the form of dreams, visions, as well as other auditory and visual perceptions together with the ability to interpret the sometimes hidden and symbolic languages in which these appear. These too are understood as communications from the unseen realm intended for the benefit and well-being of this seen one.

Ritual

As discussed in chapter 2, in African life and thought, ritual is central to the connectivity between the seen and the unseen realms of existence that is crucial for health and well-being within community. Rituals of various kinds are the language of the unseen realm expressed in the seen. As such the correct practice of appropriate ritual conveys the knowledge of the unseen into the seen. The unseen realm communicates with the seen world through ritual. What is communicated are the specific actions, activities, and materials that will effect the desired cures or healing.

Symbol

These communications are frequently in symbols that are deciphered by adepts well-versed in interpreting the messages of the unseen world. Healing is a matter of seeing and hearing—in other words, receiving and interpreting what is conveyed symbolically.

Movement and Rhythm

Anthropologist Kathryn Linn Geurts engaged in ethnographic studies among the Anlo-Ewe peoples of southeastern Ghana.

She has written extensively about *seselelame*, a term in the Anlo language that her informants frequently used. Geurts learns that seselelame, a word impossible to neatly translate into English, refers to various kinds of sensory embodiment. She writes:

> On the one hand, it seems to refer to a specific sense or kind of physical sensation that we might call tingling in the skin (sometimes a symptom of impending illness), but in other instances it is used to describe sexual arousal, heartache, or even passion.
>
> In other contexts, it refers to a kind of inspiration (to dance or to speak), but it can also be used to describe something akin to intuition (when unsure of exactly how you are coming by some information).
>
> Finally, people used it to refer to a generalized (almost synesthetic) *feeling in or through the body*, and it was proposed by some as a possible translation for the English term *sense*.[16]

Geurts learned of other ways in which Anlo-Ewe people sense or receive messages that could be described as "extrasensory perception," intuition, or premonition. She says, "they spoke of hearing a message or hearing information not through their ears but throughout their entire being, they somehow 'knew something' but could not really account for how they knew it."[17]

This "sixth sense" of *knowing through the body* was common knowledge and experience of the African people.[18]

Rhythmic bodily movement, as previously discussed, is often the form that the manifestation of spiritual entities takes. Each entity manifests its presence in specific bodily movements.[19] Bodily movement, then, is a vehicle that transmits knowledge. African traditional healers utilize their knowledge of body language in both diagnostic and therapeutic treatment of patients in their care. They discern the presence of spiritual entities as well as messages from the unseen world in the rhythmic movement of human bodies. They often prescribe forms of movement, including dance and ritual performance, to correct what may have gone wrong in the souls, spirits, and bodies of their clients.[20]

Varieties of Health Care Venues

Michael et al.'s interdisciplinary research project "Triangulated Health and Integrative Wellness"[21] highlighted a long-recognized socioeconomic reality throughout the continent of Africa and among African communities worldwide. The plain fact is that there are a plethora of sites and spaces available to the African who experiences illness of whatever kind. These venues are by no means equally equipped or resourced to deal with all conditions. The strength of this plurality lies in the potential for integration rather than competition among them. Although informal cross-referrals have gone on for decades, more formal ones are gradually becoming more widespread.

Professor Afe Adogame in the foreword to the collection of essays arising out of Michael et al.'s project writes, "Through a multi-sited ethnography in Nigeria and Ghana, the project set out to examine the integrative character in the quest for wellness and health in modern Africa through the triangulation of traditional healing shrines, medical hospitals and healing churches, which benefitted from immense popular patronage." Adogame makes clear that "their working hypothesis was that an important collaboration already existed between these triangulated domains. They identified culturally constructed beliefs and values that allowed the appropriations of wellness on multiple levels of health negotiation, and they demonstrated how and to what extent the integrative outcomes of their research had beneficial impacts and institutional significance to the holistic operations and cultural shaping of pastoral/medical practices in contemporary Africa."[22]

I would elaborate by expanding the three venues cited in the study into the following five as operative sites of healing and health care in Africa today:

1. Shrines (traditional medicine, herbal knowledge)
2. Western scientific hospitals
3. Clinics, health posts, community centers
4. African Independent churches (also known as "spiritual" churches)
5. Pentecostal/charismatic churches

The second factor identified by Michael and Danfulani in the African quest for healing is the significance of traditional shrines, discussed in the next section.

Shrines: "Powerhouses of African Spirituality"

In almost every rural community on the African continent, one can find a traditional ritual space or shrine. These, by far, are the most widespread and accessible to local, especially rural communities across Africa. These sacred spaces (e.g. shrines, groves, forests) derive their power from being inhabited or visited regularly by a spirit/deity/angel/god. Known locally as places where practitioners of the classic religious arts and rituals of African religion are typically found, they are also known to be repositories of herbal and therapeutic knowledge.

Michael and Danfulani's edited volume is a compilation of several essays that extensively explore several themes emerging from the interdisciplinary project on the centrality of African healing shrines in the mapping of African spirituality and the attainment of wellness.[23] The editors write, "these different studies underscore the continuous significance and the eternal relevance of African healing shrines as the powerhouse of African spiritualities."[24]

Malidoma Somé has written about shrines as the spaces to which Africans resort in their quest for healing. "Many traditional oriented Africans on the continent and throughout the diaspora feel that the source of illnesses can be known by consulting a diviner. After one's energy is restored, the priest or healer will repair the spiritual state so that the spiritual healing can be translated into healing of the physical disease. You have to heal in the Spirit World before you can in the physical world."[25]

The Vocation to the Practice of African Traditional Medicine

Healers are chosen or "elected" by a spirit, associated with a shrine or healing community, to the office and function of healing within community.[26] There are various ways in which this calling to the function of traditional healing is received. Typically, it is evidenced by a manifestation of spirit or deity ("possession"), which, as we have seen, always serves to enhance the relationship between the _seen_ and the _unseen_ realms of existence.

Some people are born with exceptional gifts and are endowed from birth with "spiritual power," insight, or discernment, which enables them to be agents of healing. This is an indication of having inherited the role from ancestors. Others receive their calling through a crisis experience such as a dream, vision, journey in spirit, or physical travel, such as walking through the jungle to places unknown, in which spirit is manifest. For others the calling comes through special healing from an intractable illness that inexplicably affected the individual. It is also believed that a disability or deformity may signal the election to the office or the activities of traditional healing.

Traditional Medical Specialists

As the late professor and public health researcher Kofi Appiah-Kubi carefully outlined, there are various specialties in traditional medical practice.[27] Among the Akan peoples of West Africa the following seven types of traditional medical practitioners are identified.

Herbalists (in Akan, *dunsifuor*). These are people with a knowledge of or an ability to perceive herbs, roots, fruits in which there is energy ("vital force") to overcome, reverse, or cure specific ailments.

My mother, Doris, frequently told me how my church-planting grandfather, Christian A. Doku, totally committed to the health of his community as he would often visit the herbalists and traditional medicine people in the villages and towns in which he preached, to converse with them and learn of their work with herbs in treating the sick.

These traditional herbalists, referred to in Michael and Danfulani's work as those versed in the desired experimentation in ethnopharmacopeia and locally sourced remedies, have been the most sought after by most Africans seeking healing. As noted earlier, ongoing Western scientific analysis of their herbal remedies is validating much of their work and providing much data for pharmacological research.

Diviners. These are the diagnosticians who are able to pinpoint the sources and causes of the diseases, typically through divining or contact with the unseen realms.

Movement specialists. These are the *akomfo,* or "dancers of the gods," who typically dance and make music under the inspiration of spiritual entities and thereby receive and transmit messages from the unseen world. They are drummers, dancers, and orators able to embody the interconnectedness between the natural (physical) and the unseen, ancestral realms.

Priests (in Akan, *abosomfo,* literally "people of the deities"). These are ritual practitioners, teachers, and officiants at rituals, communal festivals, or ceremonies. Though the inspiration for their work comes from the spiritual entities of the unseen realm, abosomfo, unlike akomfo, typically do not manifest the presence of the spirits by dancing, bodily movements, or spirit manifestation." Abosomfo may deliver oracles verbally but tend to be the officiants and performers of the rituals at public ceremonies.

Traditional birth attendants. These are typically women who specialize in all maternity needs, maternal, and pediatric health care.

Bonesetters. These traditional healers are orthopedic specialists with expertise in repairing broken limbs, arthritis, and rheumatism.

Exorcists or dispellers of evil spirits. Appiah-Kubi writes concerning these people that they have "come to be known in the literature as [the] *witchdoctor*" whose main function "is to exorcise the evil spirit, ward off a curse or spell, and at times, 'catch the witch.'"[28]

Public health researcher, the late Professor Isaac Sindiga, who taught at Moi University in Kenya, conducted extensive field research in traditional medicine and medical pluralism in Kenya. Sindiga observed many instances of medical pluralism there. He writes:

> Many African communities categorize disease and illness according to cause. This in turn may influence therapy-seeking and selecting behaviour. Patients will go to biomedical facilities when their families, friends or neighbours, or even themselves, believe that an illness is naturalistic—they will turn to traditional healers when they conceive an illness to be caused by human-induced forces. However, when faced with actual illness, patients in the African context have been observed to be quite flexible, sometimes using a number of systems together for the same episode of illness.[29]

Disease Is Caused by Multiple Factors

Sindiga and many other researchers have commented on the widespread understanding among Africans that diseases are caused by many different factors. These factors are identified in the somatic, spiritual, constitutional, and genetic makeup, as well as in the social and cultural environment.

For instance, the Luo people of North, East, and Central Africa believe that illness and disease may be caused through at least five different ways: air, water, and food; human causation;

the "living dead" (ancestors); inheritance; and breach of taboos or customs.[30]

Air, Water, and Food

The Luo understand that disease can be caused by air, water and food, coming from "bad air" (including weather changes and wind patterns), drinking dirty water, and eating contaminated food. Poor diet is also recognized as a health hazard.

Human Causation

Luo people also believe in human-caused disease. In this case evil people within a community may direct harm at their enemies using sorcery and witchcraft. "Witchcraft," in this usage, as previously discussed, refers to all aspects of the use of mystical power to harm others. As regards this, Luo witchcraft may be inborn, inherited, or acquired by undergoing special ceremonies and rites. The Luos, nevertheless, understand that there is also "good or beneficial magic" where mystical power is manipulated by the healer in the treatment process for the good of society. In all cases of illness caused by human agency, as in the other forms of illness causation, the Luo, like many other Africans, believe that traditional healers can neutralize the power of witches and others who may seek to do damage to persons and communities.

The Ancestors, or the "Living Dead"

The Luo believe that disease may be caused by the failure to maintain and "lubricate" vertical relationships between the human family and the ancestors. Relationship with the ancestors is kept active by remembering them, calling on them through prayers and libation, and performing ritual sacrifices for them. The ancestors are closer to God and can intercede successfully between humans and God. If the living ignore or refuse to maintain the relationships, then the ancestors may refuse to pray for the living, resulting in disease, illness, and misfortune. Ancestors may, via dreams and/or illness, make certain demands of or reveal impending challenges to the living.

Disease Inheritance

People can and do suffer illnesses that are passed down generationally. The Luo believe that certain diseases (e.g., epilepsy, some mental disturbances) are genetically transmitted to offspring.

Breach of Taboos and Customs

Breaching taboos or customs results in illness and misfortune to the offending person or family. Customs and taboos are believed to be communications from the unseen world of concretizations of sacrality or toxicity. For this reason, they are to be observed or else left alone lest their embedded power be unleashed to the detriment of the human community.

African Healing as Spiritual Care

The practice of health care and healing in classic African communal and religious contexts requires thorough diagnosis. The firm belief is that diagnosis needs to pursue the source and origins of the illness being treated. In African contexts, diagnosis, to be truly thorough, must include the physical as well as the spiritual sources of disease. African psychology and pharmacology address the source of illness not simply in terms of biological disorders. African priest-healers frequently discern illness as a manifestation of disharmony that occurs when one's *chi* (personal spirit) or *ori* ("head," or personal guiding soul) is blocked or under attack. Indigenous African pharmacology is premised on the theory that human beings are primarily spiritual creatures who temporarily reside in a material body. Healing can be achieved only when one's true form is first healed in the spirit world. Malidoma Somé goes to the heart of African spiritual care practice, writing of Dagara traditional medical practice:

> It is the duty of healers to contact the spiritual realm, which is the only way that human beings can be assured of complete healing. Healers who bring energy from the Spirit World through the gateways are known as gatekeepers. A gatekeeper can trace the shadow from this world back to its origin in the spiritual world and act as an intermediary, as a bridge since he or she understands the relationship between the different aspects of the reality of this world.[31]

Classic African religion basically operates to maintain communal and cosmic harmony between all the forces in nature. Healing aims at rectifying any imbalance within an individual and restoring the balance that is needed for good health. As such, for healing to happen it is necessary, first, to reestablish harmony between the major elements that constitute the human person. Such healing will not be complete if it does not at the same time restore harmonious relations with the environment, the divine Being, spiritual entities, ancestors, as well as other human persons.

In Critique of African Traditional Medicine

By way of critique of African traditional medicine and health care practice, following are some of the values that are recognized.

African traditional medicine has been and continues as an integral part of African culture developed over millennia. African medical practice is in keeping with the spiritual assumptions that underlie the worldview. It therefore enjoys social acceptability, even though Western scientific medicine and the Christian and Islamic faiths have made significant inroads in undermining this.

African traditional medicine tends to be holistic in approach, with disease being viewed as disequilibrium of social groups with the total environment. In this sense the traditional approach has many resonances with the message of practitioners of public health in their attention to ecological and social environments. African practice is "scientific" in the sense that it is based on years of observation and experimentation.

Part of its social acceptability results from the close relationship that exists between the traditional priest-healers and the communities in which their shrines and practice are located. Traditional priests most often are members of their community and operate within proximity of each community member. The economic factor is also very salient. African traditional medicine is affordable by the average member of the local community. Community members do not have to travel long distances to be seen by strangers who have no relationship with them and pay exorbitant amounts for treatment.

On the side of challenges, World Health Organization studies and Western medical experts point to the following five areas:

1. African traditional medicine typically does not keep up with Western scientific and technological advancement.
2. Its treatments lack "measured" doses of drugs; sometimes the side effects of the herbal remedies are unknown.
3. Its methods, techniques, training, and medicines are often kept secret.
4. It relies on the "intangible" and in some respects is based on spiritual and moral principles that are difficult to explain.
5. It is difficult to evaluate.

Thankfully each of these areas of concern is receiving attention within the guilds and communities of practice of African traditional medicine. With increasing collaboration between universities, research institutions, and traditionalists across the continent, there is hope for the benefits of integrative medicine on the African continent and its diaspora to be realized.

Conclusion

Classic African thought views health as entailing harmonious relations throughout the entire cosmos. Health care practitioners within these contexts seek to uphold and promote harmonious relations within individual as well as communal systems. Their quest is for relational holism within and between humans and the entire force fields of existence. Recognizing various potential sources of illness, they also draw on a variety of sources, material as well as spiritual, in their arts and sciences of healing and health promotion.

Notes

1. "Damfo," in Akan means "friend."
2. The name of a river in Ghana.
3. Taken from Ayi Kwei Armah, *The Healers* (Heinemann, 2000), 94–98 (my italics).
4. Matthew Michael and Umar Habila Dadem Danfulani, eds., *African Healing Shrines and Cultural Psychologies* (Regnum, 2020), 2.
5. Michael and Danfulani, *African Healing Shrines*, 2.
6. Michael and Danfulani, *African Healing Shrines*, 3.
7. Michael and Danfulani, *African Healing Shrines*, 4.
8. See, for example, J. Kwabena Asamoah-Gyadu, *Sighs and Signs of the Spirit* (Wipf & Stock, 2015).
9. Michael and Danfulani, *African Healing Shrines*, 4.
10. Michael and Danfulani, *African Healing Shrines*, 4.
11. See, for example, M. Fawzi Mahomoodally, "Traditional Medicines in Africa: An Appraisal of Ten Potent African Medicinal Plants," *Evidence-Based Complementary and Alternative Medicine* (December 3, 2013): 1–14.
12. See Bryn Trevelyan James, "'The Spirit of the Plant': Exotic Ethnopharmacopeia Among Healers in Accra, Ghana," *Anthropology Matters* 16, no. 1 (2015): 28–71.

13. World Health Organization (WHO), "Traditional, Complementary, and Integrative Medicine," https://www.who.int/health-topics/traditional-complementary-and-integrative-medicine#tab=tab_1, accessed August 16, 2025.

14. O. Ampofo and J. D. Johnson-Romauld. "Traditional Medicine and Its Role in the Development of Health Services in Africa," *Background Paper for the Technical Discussions of the 25th* 26 (1978).

15. Douglas E. Thomas, *African Traditional Religion in the Modern World* (McFarland, 2013), 203.

16. Kathryn Linn Geurts, *Culture and the Senses* (University of California Press, 2002), 41.

17. Geurts, *Culture and the Senses*, 54–55.

18. For further exploration of embodied epistemologies, see Emmanuel Y. Lartey, "Knowing Through Moving: African Embodied Epistemologies," in *Sensing Sacred: Exploring the Human Senses in Practical Theology and Pastoral Care*, ed. Jennifer Baldwin (Lexington, 2016), 101–13.

19. See Kofi Appiah-Kubi, *Man Cures, God Heals: Religion and Medical Practice Among the Akans of Ghana* (Allanheld, Osman, 1981).

20. Lartey, "Knowing Through Moving," 105.

21. Matthew Michael, Hauwa Yusuf, and Nathan Chiroma, "Triangulated Health and Integrative Wellness": The Mapping of Wellness and Its Cultural Psychology in Modern Africa" (under the auspices of the Nagel Institute with generous funding by Templeton Foundation 2018–2020).

22. Afe Adogame, foreword to *African Healing Shrines & Cultural Psychologies*, eds. Matthew Michael and Umar H. D. Danfulani (Augsburg Fortress, 2020), x.

23. Michael and Danfulani, eds., *African Healing Shrines & Cultural Psychologies*, 5.

24. Michael and Danfulani, *African Healing Shrines*, 12.

25. Malidoma Patrice Somé, *Healing Wisdom of Africa: Finding Life Purpose Through Nature, Ritual, and Community* (TarcherPerigree, 1999), 73.

26. For further elaboration, see, Appiah-Kubi, *Man Cures, God Heals*, 37–40.

27. Appiah-Kubi, *Man Cures, God Heals*, 35–36.

28. Appiah-Kubi, *Man Cures, God Heals*, 36.

29. Isaac Sindiga, Chacha Nyaigotti-Chacha, and May Peter Kanunah, eds., *Traditional Medicine in Africa* (East African Educational Publishers, 1995).

30. See Isaac Sindiga, "Managing Illness Among the Luo," in *Traditional Medicine in Africa*, ed. Isaac Sindiga, Chacha Nyaigotti-Chacha, and

Mary Peter Kanunah (East African Educational Publishers, 1995), 64–79. See also Evelynes Agot Kawango, "Ethnomedical Remedies and Therapies in Maternal and Child Health Among the Rural Luo," 80–93.

31. Somé, *Healing Wisdom of Africa*, 75.

7

Death Is Like Birth

Death and Life in African Religious Cultures

IN ALL CULTURES THE FACT of death and the processes of dying evoke many different responses. Death has remained an enigma for all of humanity for as long as human beings have lived on earth. Africans have also pondered and engaged the inevitable reality of death and have elaborated a variety of beliefs, rites, rituals, and practices in response to it. In this chapter I will attempt with broad brushstrokes to indicate the general direction of many and varied African religious traditions and cultures in relation to death. It is important to reiterate the fact that is evident throughout this book, that there are myriads of peoples, cultures, and religions across the continent of Africa and in its diaspora. Africa is a vast and complex continent with opposing and contrasting views on almost any subject. Nevertheless, it is also true that there are themes and trends of thought that distinguish African cultural forms from those of other historic cultures. Attitudes, rituals, and practices surrounding death present us with an example of unity of direction of thought and practice in the midst of this complex variety. So that whereas there are very different funerary practices observable on the continent, on careful examination one begins to see how these different practices point in a common direction of thought concerning humanity, death, and life. It is to these "common directions of thought" that I wish to direct our thinking to explore how these ways of thinking about life and death might inform and inspire our interactions with each other across religious traditions and enhance our coping with the inevitable grief, pain, and loss that death entails. The overall aim here is to articulate and explore what spiritual care that arises from these African beliefs and practices around death looks like.

Life Has No Opposite: Death Is a Doorway

In many non-African traditions life ends with death. Death in these cultures is the "opposite," negation, or termination of life. Death brings life to an end and is therefore the enemy, opponent, or opposer of life. Put differently, just like the opposite of hot is cold, of youth is old age, of male is female, of wise is foolish, of physical is spiritual, so the opposite of life is death. In many Western cultures, for instance, death is seen as the termination of life. Death is therefore to be feared, hated, avoided or else postponed for as long as possible. Death in these cultures is literally <u>the <u>*worst thing*</u></u> that could happen to a person.

In African life and thought, on the contrary, life has no opposite. Death is not the opposite of life. Life has no opposite or ultimate termination. Life never ends. Life continues in many different ways and in a variety of forms. Existence remains. Human beings transition from one state or form of existence to another. In this African sense, if there is an opposite of death it is not life but rather, birth. Birth, like an entry door, ushers us into the form of existence we call earthly life, and death, like an exit door, ushers us out of life as we know it and into another form of life variously called spiritual, unseen, invisible, heavenly, the after-life, the place of the dead, or in the land of the spirits. Sociologist and professor emeritus Kofi Asare Opoku writes, "West Africans regard death not as the end of life, but as a transition from this present earthly life to another life in the land of the spirits."[1] Existence is conceived of as taking place in essentially two locales, forms or realms—the seen, visible, physical realm, "earthly" *wiadzie mu* (Akan); and the unseen, invisible, spiritual realm, "spiritual" *samanadzie* in Akan. Each of these realms is complex, containing many different sites and forms of life. Just as there are many forms, locations, and stations in earthly life, so also there are in the spiritual realm. Moreover, these two realms are not far away from each other but rather are in communion and communication with each other. What happens in one realm can have consequences in the other. Humans pass between these two worlds through the portals of birth and death.

A Gikuyu informant of Maryknoll missionary and anthropologist Michael Kirwen expressed it this way: "Death is a rite of passage just as initiation and birth. Death is the separation of people who die physically from those who are living but still together in spirit."[2] For an Akamba man, "Death and dying is a process in life, which each person has to go through. It is the process of coming from living and going to the next stage of the living dead."[3] A Bemba informant expressed their view: "Death is a very painful experience, and it separates people from their beloved ones. Though it is not liked by people it is a rite of passage into another world. It also transmits life into newly born infants."[4]

Dying Is a Journey

Emeritus professor John Mbiti in his classic study *African Religions and Philosophy*[5] presents several terms used in different African languages to describe the act of dying. The Basoga of Uganda say of a person who has died that they have "gone," "gone down to the grave," "our friend was told by death to tie up his load and go." Among the Abaluyia (of Kenya, Uganda, and Tanzania), dying is described as "going to the place of the dead," "going home," or "looking for an exit." The Akamba (of Kenya) use, among others, terms meaning "to follow the company of one's grandparents," "to go home," "to be fetched or summoned," "to be called," "to be received or taken away," "to return back," "to depart or go," "to go where other people have gone," or "to leave, forsake or abandon." Mbiti explains that for a person who dies at an early age the expression used is "to have a miscarriage," thus drawing attention to similarities between death and birth in African conceptualizing.

Among the Akans of Ghana and Côte D'Ivoire, as declared by Binghamton University professor of religion Dr. Anthony Ephirim-Donkor, "the elders, particularly kings and queen mothers, never die, but merely travel to other villages."[6] In fact, the announcement of the death of a chief or a queen mother is, among the Akans and the Gã-Dangbes of Ghana, invariably couched in terms of a royal journey: "Nana (the King or Queen) has traveled to the Village."

The Chagga (of Kenya and Tanzania) understand that the journey from this world to the other takes nine days. The journey is hazardous since the soul must travel through a dangerous wilderness.[7] Mbiti, at points following Goody, whose ethnographic work in Northern Ghana is well regarded, explains that the LoDagaa (Dagari) peoples of Northern Ghana believe that the "land of the departed" lies to the west of their geographical location as a people, and that it is separated from them by the "river of Death."[8] Once funeral rites have been performed, the LoDagaa understand, the soul begins its journey. At the river it is ferried or canoed across, for a fee of twenty cowries that friends and relatives provide at the funeral. Several African groups engage in the practice of providing money or other essentials, at times placed in the casket, to be used for transportation fees across the river. To the LoDagaa the crossing of this river is an ordeal, the difficulty of which depends on how the deceased lived. Moral and upright people cross over with little difficulty; immoral, wicked, or corrupt people have great difficulty and may even fall out of the canoe and have to swim across, a task that may take up to three years to complete. Goody explains that "it is debtors, thieves, witches and those who denied something to others that face the greatest difficulties in either being allowed to cross or in the act of crossing the river."[9] On arrival at the other end the soul must be welcomed and admitted into the new order by the older ancestors.

The Gã peoples of southeastern Ghana have a ritual that symbolizes and mystically enacts this river crossing. Led by the eldest child of the deceased followed in order of birth by the other children and directed by the officiating priest, family members simulate the action of oarsmen in a canoe bearing the deceased across the river. With an appropriate song that the priest leads in singing, and often accompanied by drumming, the family members symbolically and ritually carry their parent into the land of the dead in this way. The belief is that this ritual needs to be performed correctly for the journey of the deceased to be successfully completed. Without it the deceased remains an earthbound spirit that may in its frustration torment these selfsame family members.

Burial Rites

Funerary processes, rituals, and body disposal rites reveal much about a people's beliefs about death. Rituals, rites, and burial practices all attest to the understanding that death, far from being an end, is rather a journey to a different realm. As Kofi Asare Opoku explains, since death is not the end or termination of a person's life, it does not sever their connections with family. Rather, death extends the family relationships into infinity and eternity. The ceremonies and rituals performed by the living for the dead emphasize the unbroken family relationship between the living who inhabit the seen realm and the dead who inhabit the unseen realm of existence. The African family, as such, has an eternal and spiritual quality to it, "being made up of both the living and the dead, [and] the reality of the continued membership of the departed is shown by the consideration given it in every family activity"[10]—eating meals, whenever the family or community gathers for any discussion or other purpose, in times of dispute and conflict, ceremonies, rites of passage, and so on. In every family activity, recognition and acknowledgment are given to the ancestors. Opoku explains that the living and the dead both have parts to play in fulfilling family responsibilities. Things go well for a family when both sides perform their obligations properly. A major responsibility of the living is the performance of proper and fitting funeral rites for the dead of the family. Thereafter they are to "offer them sacrifices, food and drink which constitute acts of remembrance and reverence."[11] The dead on their part play an important role in human society and in the life of their families because their existence on a higher, limitless plane beyond this world gives them increased power. "Their role," says Opoku, "is to protect, direct, intervene and guide their families, and also to serve as elders [i.e., inspired leaders, conflict transformation experts, healers, doctors,] of the family."[12]

Burial is almost universally the chosen means of disposal of the body. National laws together with the establishment of designated spaces of land as cemeteries, enacted in the colonial era, currently dictate the location of burials. However, in some cultures a corpse is customarily buried within the house where the deceased was living at the time of death. In other cultures, burials take place within the compound where a person's home is located. Yet others bury their dead "at the place where the person was born"[13] or where their umbilical cord was buried at birth.[14]

Graves differ in shape and size, with some being rectangular, others circular, and some having cave-like or bunk-like shapes at the end where several corpses of a family may be laid to rest.[15]

Proverbial Coffins

The Gã peoples of Teshie, Ghana, have recently perfected the craft of burying their dead in elaborate, artfully constructed caskets customized to exemplify the deceased's personality, family group symbol or totem, or occupation or station in life. I have personally performed burials where the casket was shaped in the form of an elephant (family totem), an airplane (for a pilot), a

Mercedes-Benz (for a businessman), and an eagle. These fantasy or figurative coffins also called *custom*, *fantastic*, or *proverbial coffins* (in Gã, *abɛbuu adekai*), are functional caskets made by specialized carpenters. Developed out of the figurative palanquins in which royals ride into state on festive occasions, they are not only coffins but are considered real works of art. Further, they have cosmic or spiritual significance. The significance lies in their depicting, enacting, and signaling to the next world the status, manner of life, dignity, and industriousness of the one who is now entering that world. The hope and aim of the family are to say to the ancestral realm, "Here comes our great illustrious family member, receive her or him and accord them the same dignity and status that befits them just as we have afforded them in our realm." This honoring of ancestors reverberates through the whole created order. It shows to the living as well as the dead a family's respect for the one who has died.

Samanadzie (the Place of the Dead)

No other civilization is on record to have done as much to preserve and celebrate the dead as the Ancient Egyptians. These ancient Africans developed elaborate funerary rites for their deceased kings, priests, seers, teachers, and ordinary folk. The Akans for their part refer to the place to which all who die proceed as *samanadzie* or *asamando*. Gãs refer to it as *gbohiiadje*. To the Akans samanadzie is reserved exclusively for all those who die—whether one believes in it or not. It is set aside for those who suffer physical death, and so other spirits (e.g., deities, nature spirits, etc.), since they do not die, do not typically inhabit samanadzie. In samanadzie there are separate worlds for the ancestors (*nananom nsamanfo*) and ordinary citizens (*nsamanfo*). Ephirim-Donkor correctly explains the Akan saying "Nyipa wo berbi ko" (literally "a person has somewhere to go") as having two meanings—teleological and ethical.[16] Teleologically, it refers to the fact of destiny, purposefulness, and goals in life and for living. Earthly life has a destiny or

destination. We are headed in life in the direction of samanadzie. Ethically, it is an injunction to live one's life on earth
in such a way as to ensure an honored place (ancestorhood) in
the world to come. It enjoins a quality of life that will please
one's ancestors, uplift one's community, and ensure a place of
honor for one in the spiritual realm upon death.

Ancestors, Elders, and Spirits

In a careful explanation of differences between ancestors
(human) and *abosom* (spirits), Ephirim-Donkor writes, "The
Ancestors, including the *Nsamanfo*, do not enter the sphere of
the *Abosom*, but only the Nananom Nsamanfo (ancestors) make
periodic visits to the abode of the primeval *Abosom*, while the
Nsamanfo visit the *Abosom* per invitations only."[17] Ephirim-
Donkor further offers a telling indication of the closeness of
images of birth and death in Akan religious thought.
"Symbolically," he asserts, "the Samanadzie is emblematic of the
womb." A dark and dreaded place, it, like the womb, is also a
place of tremendous power, nurture, and spectacular energy not
to be toyed with, the source of all that exists in the mundane
world. In keeping with Akan matrilineal and matrifocal practice and thought, "the ruler of Samanadzie is a woman, the
NaSaman." "The NaSaman sends her offspring into the corporeal Wiadzie from Samanadzie to achieve eldership existentially
in order to live as ancestors."[18]

All that are born into the corporeal world are destined to
reenter the samanadzie upon death as *nsamanfo*. However, a
small number of the dead—known as *atofo*—who suffered vio-
lent, sudden, or tragic deaths, defer entering the *samanadzie* due
to the nature and circumstance of death. Because they were denied the chance to fulfil their *nkrabea* (soul's life purpose and
plan negotiated with the Creator before birth), they may reas-
sume human form and live lives far removed from their relatives
or else may continue living as agitated and vengeful spirits in
limbo.

Elders (*nananom npanyifo* in Akan) are living human beings who have achieved the highest social, spiritual, and ethical status of a community's ideals. Says Ephirim-Donkor, "An elder is that generative individual who masters the secrets and arts of living. After living an altruistic life, marrying and having children, and living a productive life of giving back to the community that first nurtured and sustained the individual the same community now confers on the generative individual the title of elder."[19] The community sees in the elder qualities and attributes that said society deems beneficial to its well-being and survival. It is elders who, on entrance, welcome and settling into samanadzie, become ancestors.

Names and Naming of the Newborn: The Return of the Dead

In many African cultures the dead—or perhaps better "enlivening spirits" of the dead—are believed to return to earth to be reborn into their families. In what may be described as a partial reincarnation, it is essentially dominant characteristics and the spirit of the ancestor that are believed to be reincarnated in particular descendants. This is so because as Opoku declares, "each soul remains distinct and each birth represents a new soul, and even though the ancestor is believed to be re-incarnated in his [or her] grandchildren or great-grandchildren, he [or she] nevertheless continues to live in the afterlife."[20]

This "partial reincarnation" of ancestors is expressed and reenacted in the custom of naming children after their grandparents and other ancestors. Several examples of this practice can be given: The Akan name Ababio literally means "the one has returned or come again." The Yoruba have several names that point to the return of ancestors: Iyabo, Mother has returned; *Yetunde,* Mother comes a second time; and Babatunde, Father has returned. The Ewes of Southeastern Ghana, Togo, and Benin give names such as Afetogbo, meaning "the master has come back again," to children born after the death of a family member. Degbo̲, gone and returned; Evavakpo̲, he has ventured to return; and Noviegbo̲, sister has come back again. In this African view, the name a person is given significantly influences their life. It is therefore the names of illustrious and inspiring ancestors that are given. Ephirim-Donkor captures it well when he writes: "To have a name is to have a soul and vice versa. Therefore, as long as the dead are remembered, the ancestors, though dead, are alive and well. Actually, the names of the dead are that which survived death, and depending on how powerful those names or souls are, they influence the course of events for their living descendants."[21]

A special bond exists between grandparents and their grandchildren among the Gã peoples, partly because the Gã naming system revolves around sets of names that are repeated every other generation. As such, grandparents have the same sets of names—which are constructed around gender and birth order—as their grandchildren.

Grief and the Care of the Bereaved

Dagara traditional philosopher/healer Malidoma Somé, in *Ritual: Power, Healing and Community*, presents a telling insider's account of grieving and its place in Dagara (Burkina Faso) community. He declares, "If death disturbs the living, it offers a unique opportunity to unleash one of the strongest emotional powers humans have: the power to grieve."[22] For the Dagara, a people who do not know how to weep together cannot truly laugh together. "People who know not the power of shedding their tears together are like a time bomb, dangerous to themselves and to the world around them."[23] The Dagara, Somé argues, understand the expression of emotion as a process of self-rekindling or calming, which not only helps in handling death but also resets and repairs the feelings within a person.

Grief, according to Somé and in line with the expressions of many traditionalists I have interviewed, is in fact *owed to the dead* as one of the things that can help complete the death process. Writes Somé, "Grief delivers to the dead **that which they need** to travel to the realm of the dead—a release of emotional energy that also provides a sense of completion or endedness, closure. This sense of closure is also needed by the griever who has to let go of the person who has died" (emphases in original).[24] For the Dagara, grief is like food for the psyche. Just as the body needs food, so the psyche needs grief to maintain its own healthy balance.

Funerals, therefore, have a very prominent place and role in the social life of most African communities. Much of communal life revolves around rituals and ceremonies associated with the commemoration of death and the dead. Grief, especially the expression and ritualizing of grief, is a deeply significant aspect of African social life. Death, as we have seen, is not seen as an ending but rather as an opportunity for a person to "take off these ragged clothes we call a body and walk naked."[25] Yet death does produce a sudden vacuum and loss of closeness and attachment that requires grief to heal. Without the expression and ventilation of grief, the separation between the living and the dead is never complete. The living on their part are unable to accept the fact that a loved one has departed this realm and entered the spiritual realm. The departed on their part are unable to arrive at their destination in the spiritual realm because they lack the emotional energy of the grief of the living they need to propel them into that realm. The departed consequentially may become angry with the living. Thus, if there is no expression of grief, it will affect both the dead and the living detrimentally. The dead are unable to travel free from their earth consciousness. They remain tied down to an earthly consciousness—and "may begin to intrude into the business of the living in a way that can constitute a serious nuisance."[26]

Spiritual Care in Times of Death and Bereavement

Implications that flow from African conceptualizing of death as a form of birth are many. Following are seven that seem to me to have significance for spiritual care with people impacted by African life and thought.

1. *Death is to be celebrated as much as birth.* Both point to life's eternal quality. Spiritual care practitioners can help through ritual, teaching, and presence to embody and articulate the similarity of death and birth as entrance and exit gateways between parallel worlds.

2. *Death is neither to be feared, denied, nor ignored.* It, like birth, is a doorway through which all must pass to enter different realms or spheres of life. Death is a part of life. The only way to continue living is to die.

3. *Death, like birth, is painful.* Suffering is a part of entry into life in all its forms. The sufferings associated with both relate to and lead inexorably to the joys and realities of the next form of life to which one goes.

4. *It is important to make healthy and useful contributions to the community in which you live.* This is the path to ancestorhood and eternal life. Contributing to the well-being of the communities we are a part of is a form of investment into our own life beyond our exit through death.

5. *Honor your ancestors.* And they will also honor you. There is a bond between the living and the dead that needs to be respected and ritually maintained.

6. *The dead, like the newborn, depend on the living for certain important things.* Your ancestors need you as much as you need them. African traditions

have rituals of cleansing, renewal, and remembrance for the ancestors. Spiritual care providers can seek out and enact these rituals that symbolize and activate the synergy between the living and the dead.

7. *The expression of grief need not be suppressed.* In recognition of the fact that the emotional energy of grief is needed by both the living and the dead, grief must be expressed and not suppressed. For the living it is cathartic, and for the dead it provides the energy that propels them into the next life. Spiritual care providers may facilitate the ventilation of grief feelings as expressions of much-needed emotional energy, beneficial to both the living and the departed.

Notes

1. Kofi Asare Opoku, *West African Traditional Religion* (FEP International Private, 1978), 133.
2. Michael Kirwen, *African Cultural Knowledge: Themes and Embedded Beliefs* (MIAS, 2005), 248.
3. Kirwen, *African Cultural Knowledge*, 248.
4. Kirwen, *African Cultural Knowledge*, 249.
5. John S. Mbiti, *African Religions and Philosophy* (Heinemann, 1969),152.
6. Anthony Ephirim-Donkor, *African Religion Defined: A Systematic Study of Ancestor Worship Among the Akan* (Hamilton, 2016), 53.
7. Mbiti, *African Religions and Philosophy*, 155.
8. Mbiti, *African Religions and Philosophy*, 155.
9. Referred to and cited by Mbiti, *African Religions and Philosophy*, 155.
10. Opoku, *West African Traditional Religion*, 133.
11. Opoku, *West African Traditional Religion*, 133.
12. Opoku, *West African Traditional Religion*, 134.
13. Mbiti, *African Religions and Philosophy*, 154.
14. Usually under a tree.
15. Mbiti, *African Religions and Philosophy*, 154.

16. Ephirim-Donkor, *African Religion Defined*, 27.

17. Ephirim-Donkor, *African Religion Defined*, 28. *Nananom nsamanfo* are those humans who in death have achieved the status of ancestors. *Nsamanfo* are "ordinary" dead humans, namely those who have not achieved ancestral status.

18. Ephirim-Donkor, *African Religion Defined*, 28.

19. Ephirim-Donkor, *African Religion Defined*, 21.

20. Opoku, *West African Traditional Religion*, 138.

21. Ephirim-Donkor, *African Religion Defined*, 51.

22. Malidoma Patrice Somé, *Ritual: Power, Healing and Community* (Penguin Compass, 1997), 72.

23. Somé, *Ritual*, 73.

24. Somé, *Ritual*, 73 (my emphasis and underlining).

25. Somé, *Ritual*, 73.

26. Somé, *Ritual*, 74.

8

Tsamō: African Spiritual Care

I T HAS RIGHTLY BEEN SUGGESTED that the primary
goal and aim of classic African religion is none other
than spiritual care.[1] Practitioners and adepts of classic
African religion affirm that they practice and receive forms of
spiritual care through the rituals, practices, and activities of
their faith. The ultimate and overall aim of spiritual care in
classic African thought can be described as a quest for what I
would term *cosmic relational harmony*. Ultimately, the practice of spiritual care in the African religious sense is about
restoring right relations between and within the realms of existence. African practitioners declare through word and ritual
that things are wrong in the human realm because of disharmony within and between the realms. Classic African spiritual care providers operate to restore relationships and let
broken chords vibrate once again throughout the whole created order.

In Gã language the term for healing is *tsamō*. The literal
meaning of tsamō is "putting together," "uniting," or "reconciling." The meaning therefore is that in healing, one puts
things together that have become separated. Healing implies
bringing together estranged parties. For the Gã, illness, disease,
or disharmony is the result of separation between spirit and
body, the visible and the invisible realms, the material and the
immaterial. The deepest and most important work of the Gã
spiritual care provider is reconciling these estranged dimensions
of our human experience.

This is to say that the purpose and function of practices of spiritual care within African religious contexts is ultimately healing and restoration of relationships on a cosmic scale.

Douglas Thomas draws on the work of Malidoma Somé when he writes:

> It is the traditional rituals which many Europeans consider barbaric that black people must employ to restore harmony and the lost centuries that the colonial locust and canker worms have eaten. The African psyche is severely damaged and remains under assault from acts of barbarism and white supremacy. Thus, the African collective can be healed only by addressing their relationships with the visible worlds of nature, community, and the invisible forces of the ancestors and Spirit allies. For it is in ritual that nature, community, and the Spirit World come together to support the inner building of identity.[2]

What must by now be clear to us all is that (1) *restoration of harmony* in community, (2) addressing of *relationships with the visible worlds* of nature and community, and (3) healing relationships with *the invisible forces of the ancestors* and spiritual entities are the three principal functions of African spiritual care. Moreover, *ritual,* as we have discussed it throughout this text, is the principal means employed by African spiritual care practitioners to bring this about.

Restoration of Harmony

Healing of Persons

Unlike in Western thought where the *psyche* (soul, mind) is perceived as central in definitions of personhood and in the healing of the maladies of humanity, *spirituality* is what lies at the heart of African anthropology and relationality is core to personhood. African spirituality is a way of life that sees the human's spirit as central and key to health and well-being. African religion is not like the fancy clothes we put on to attend worship services and take off afterward. Rather, it is like the skin in which we live at all times. All earthly life pulsates with the rhythms of the invisible spiritual realm, and spirituality provides the locus and the means to address the issues of life. African spiritual care gives primacy to the human spirit. Restoration of harmony begins within the spirit of humanity.

The words of Damfo, the traditional healer in Ayi Kwei Armah's classic historical novel *The Healers*, from which we drew many thoughts about African traditional healing in chapter 6, captures the essence of African spiritual care for all persons: "*The Healing [of] an individual person—what is that but restoring a lost unity to that individual's body and spirit?*"[3]

Disease results from disharmony between the facets of one's personhood. African spiritual care aims essentially at restoring harmonious relationships within persons. In Akan terminology, for example, there may be conflict between one's *okra* and one's *sunsum*. Spiritual care practitioners aim, through their disciplined practices, to help diagnose the conflict and work with the individuals to figure out the most appropriate rituals that will heal the rift and restore the relationship.

Addressing Relationships with the Visible World

Comprehensive Care

Spiritual care in African contexts goes much further than the individual. It necessarily takes the shape and form of attention to body, spirit, soul, and mind, in social, economic, political, and communal settings, fully recognizing and addressing the interconnected nature of all these aspects of human life. In African spiritual care, treatment must be integrated and encompass ecological, communal, psychological, physiological, and spiritual dimensions. Solely addressing intrapsychic dimensions is insufficient to respond to the entirety of human existence, especially in the context of the communal mindsets and style of living that pervade

African consciousness. It is in addressing social, economic, political, as well as environmental factors that African spiritual care providers achieve the comprehensiveness that makes for healthy communities within which persons can flourish.

Healing Communities

People who are alienated from their spiritual roots are disconnected, rootless, and diseased. Whole communities may be disconnected from their ancestral and spiritual relations and thus become diseased. Disharmony, disconnection, and disease go together in African life and thought. It is a function of spiritual care to decipher the nature and sources of disharmony and devise communal rituals that will result in restoring relational harmony. Spiritual care from classic African philosophical and religious perspectives fosters respect for all humankind and respectful engagement with all.

Addressing Relationships with the Invisible World

Cosmic Connectivity

African spiritual care draws on the spirituality of the people. It taps into the energy of life (vital force, spiritual energy) by and within which humans live. African spiritual care practitioners intensively engage the invisible realm in their ritual practice, knowing that ritual has a transformative effect on human life. African spiritual care providers strengthen themselves and their practice by intensively engaging in those spiritual disciplines that strengthen their relationship with the unseen world. Spiritual care must *facilitate intelligent and compassionate interaction with the "spiritual powers"* for the good of all.

Malidoma Somé reminds us of the duty of healers, and therefore of all spiritual care practitioners, to *contact the spiritual realm*, which is the only way that human beings can be assured of complete healing. African spiritual care practices entail an energized openness to, awareness of, and embodied engagement with the "unseen" dimensions of existence. African spiritual care therefore revolves around the discovery and performance of appropriate rituals that unleash the power of the ancestral realm to heal and restore relationships within the living human community.

Warding Off Negativity

Practitioners of African spiritual care are keenly aware of how life energy can be manipulated and harnessed in ways that are destructive and harmful to human life. They know how to contend effectively against this harmful use of power. African spiritual care providers learn how to neutralize, counteract, or reverse the harmful spiritual forces that persons, consumed by the malevolent side of their nature, may have unleashed in a desire to harm persons. They also know how to unleash the beneficial effects of spiritual energy.

Unleashing Beneficence for All

At the end of it all, African spiritual care aims at engaging the energy of life through rituals that connect the human social sphere, nature, and the material environment, and the invisible realm of deities, ancestors, and spiritual entities, in releasing restorative and healing power into human community, and in promoting the flourishing of all creatures. This ultimately is what African spiritual care providers are summoned to by the manifestation of spiritual entities in their bodies. This is what they are trained by their spiritual elders and mentors to do for the benefit and blessing of all creation.

Notes

1. *Tsamo* is the word in my mother (and father)-tongue, the Gã language of Ghana, for "healing, joining together, or reconciling."

2. Douglas E. Thomas, *African Traditional Religion in the Modern World* (McFarland, 2013), 127–128 (with reference to Malidoma Patrice Somé, *Healing Wisdom of Africa: Finding Life Purpose Through Nature, Ritual, and Community* [TarcherPerigee, 19990], 4, 17).
3. Ayi Kwei Armah, *The Healers* (Heinemann, 1979), 98 (my italics).

BIBLIOGRAPHY

Adeyemo, Tokunboh. *Salvation in African Tradition*. Evangel, 1997.

Ampofo, O., and J. D. Johnson-Romauld. "Traditional Medicine and Its Role in the Development of Health Services in Africa." *Background Paper for the Technical Discussions of the 25th*, 26, 1978.

Appiah-Kubi, Kofi. *Man Cures, God Heals: Religion and Medical Practice Among the Akans of Ghana*. Allanheld, Osmun, 1981.

Armah, Ayi Kwei. *The Healers*. Heinemann, 1978/2000.

Aryee, Seth A. *History of the Establishment and Expansion of the Methodist Church, Ghana: Greater Accra, Eastern, Volta Regions. 1838–1978*. (Unpublished thesis).

Asamoah-Gyadu, J. Kwabena. *Sighs and Signs of the Spirit: Ghanaian Perspectives on Pentecostalism and Renewal in Africa*. Wipf & Stock, 2015.

Baldwin, Jennifer. ed. *Sensing Sacred: Exploring the Human Senses in Practical Theology and Pastoral Care*. Lexington. 2016.

Beaubrun, Mimerose P. *Nan Dòmi: An Initiate's Journey into Haitian Vodou*. Translated by D. J. Walker. City Lights, 2010.

Bray, Karen, Heather Eaton, and Whitney Bauman, eds. *Earthly Things: Immanence, New Materialisms, and Planetary Thinking*. Fordham University Press, 2023.

Clark, Rosemary. *The Sacred Magic of Ancient Egypt: The Spiritual Practice Restored*. Llewellyn, 2003.

Clark, Rosemary. *The Sacred Tradition in Ancient Egypt: The Esoteric Wisdom Revealed*. Llewellyn, 2000.

Daniel, Yvonne. *Dancing Wisdom: Embodied Knowledge in Haitian Vodou, Cuban Yoruba, and Bahian Candomblé*. University of Illinois Press, 2005.

Doumbia, Adama, and Naomi Doumbia. *The Way of the Elders: West African Spirituality and Tradition*. Llewellyn, 2004.

Ephirim-Donkor, Anthony. *African Religion Defined: A Systematic Study of Ancestor Worship Among the Akan.* University Press of America, 2013.

Geurts, Kathryn Linn. *Culture and the Senses: Bodily Ways of Knowing in an African Community.* University of California Press, 2002.

James, Bryn Trevelyan. "'The Spirit of the Plant': Exotic Ethnopharmacopeia Among Healers in Accra, Ghana." *Anthropology Matters* 16, no. 1 (2015): 28–71.

Jefferson-Tatum, Elana. "Africana Sacred Matters: Religious Materialities in Africa, the Caribbean, and the Americas." In *Earthly Things: Immanence, New Materialisms, and Planetary Thinking*, edited by Karen Bray, Heather Eaton, and Whitney Bauman, 60–73. Fordham University Press, 2023.

Kirwen, Michael C., ed. *African Cultural Knowledge: Themes and Embedded Beliefs.* MIAS, 2005.

Lartey, Emmanuel Y. *In Living Color: An Intercultural Approach to Pastoral Care and Counseling.* Jessica Kingsley, 2003.

Lartey, Emmanuel Y. *Pastoral Theology in an Intercultural World.* Wipf & Stock, 2013.

Lartey, Emmanuel Y. *Postcolonializing God: An African Practical Theology.* SCM Press, 2013.

Lartey, Emmanuel Y., and Hellena Moon, eds. *Postcolonial Images of Spiritual Care: Challenges of Care in a Neoliberal Age.* Pickwick, 2020.

Magesa, Laurenti. *African Religion: The Moral Traditions of Abundant Life.* Orbis, 1997.

Magesa, Laurenti. *What Is Not Sacred? African Spirituality.* Orbis, 2013.

Mahomoodally, M. Fawzi. "Traditional Medicines in Africa: An Appraisal of Ten Potent African Medicinal Plants." *Evidence-Based Complementary and Alternative Medicine* (2013): 1–14.

Mawere, Munyaradzi. *African Belief and Knowledge Systems: A Critical Perspective.* Langaa Research & Publishing Common Initiative Group, 2011.

Mbiti, John S. *African Religions and Philosophy.* Heinemann, 1990.

Michael, Matthew, and Umar Habila Dadem Danfulani, eds. *African Healing Shrines and Cultural Psychologies.* Regnum, 2020.

Mutwa, Vusamazulu Credo. *Zulu Shaman: Dreams, Prophecies, and Mysteries.* Destiny, 2003.

Ndubisi, E. J. O. "The Notion of Satan/Ekwensu: A Comparative Study of Western and African (Igbo) Thoughts." *OWIJOPPA* 3, no. 1. (2019), ISSN (Online) 2630–7057, 23–36.

Opoku, Kofi Asare. *West African Traditional Religion.* FEP International, 1978.

Orobator, Agbonkhianmeghe E. *Religion and Faith in Africa: Confessions of an Animist*. Orbis, 2018.

Oyeronke Oyewumi. *The Invention of Women: Making an African Sense of Western Gender Discourses*. University of Minneapolis Press, 1997.

P'Bitek, Okot. *Decolonizing African Religions: A Short History of African Religions in Western Scholarship*. Diasporic Africa Press, 2011.

Pobee, John S. *Toward an African Theology*. Abingdon, 1979.

Sindiga, Isaac, Chacha Nyaigotti-Chacha, and Mary Peter Kanunah, eds. *Traditional Medicine in Africa*. East African Educational Publishers, 1995.

Somé, Malidoma Patrice. *The Healing Wisdom of Africa: Finding Life Purpose Through Nature, Ritual, and Community*. Jeremy P. Tarcher/ Putnam Penguin, 1998.

Somé, Malidoma Patrice. *Of Water and the Spirit: Ritual, Magic, and Initiation in the Life of an African Shaman*. Penguin Compass, 1994.

Somé, Malidoma Patrice. *Ritual: Power, Healing and Community*. Penguin Compass, 1993.

Suthers, Ellen. "Perception, Knowledge and Divination in Djimini Society, Ivory Coast." Unpublished PhD diss., University of Virginia, 1987.

Tetteh, Ishmael N. O. *New Era of Spirituality: Spirituality from the Wisdom of Nature*. Conscious Humanity Press, 2021.

Thomas, Douglas E. *African Traditional Religion in the Modern World*. McFarland, 2015.

Vega, Marta Moreno. *The Altar of My Soul: The Living Traditions of Santería*. Random House, 2000.

Walker, Sheila S. *Ceremonial Spirit Possession in Africa and Afro-America: Forms, Meanings, and Functional Significance for Individuals and Social Groups*. E. J. Brill, 1972.

INDEX

ABOUT THE AUTHOR

Emmanuel Yartekwei Lartey is the Charles Howard Candler Professor of Pastoral Theology and Spiritual Care at Emory University's Candler School of Theology. He is a distinguished faculty member in the Graduate Division of Religion and affiliate faculty in the African American Studies Department at Emory. He has held faculty positions in practical theology at the University of Birmingham in the UK and Ghana, and was previously professor of pastoral theology, care, and counseling at Columbia Theological Seminary, Decatur, GA. His book *In Living Color: An Intercultural Approach to Pastoral Care and Counseling* (2003) is used as a textbook in seminaries across the world.